bakery treats

Publications International, Ltd.

Favorite Brand Name Recipes at www.fbnr.com

Pictured on the front cover *(clockwise from top left):* Homemade Cookie Bags
(page 100), Italian Almond Cake *(page 126),* Chocolate Cherry Layer Cake
(page 132) and Ham Croissants *(page 26).*

Pictured on the back cover *(clockwise from top left):* Stamped Fruit & Vegetable
Labels *(page 56),* Lavender Cream Cake *(page 138),* Fresh Herb Wreath *(page 28)*
and Cherry Almond Biscotti *(page 98).*

ISBN: 0-7853-6683-0

Library of Congress Control Number: 2002100176

Manufactured in China.

8 7 6 5 4 3 2 1

Contents

Savory Filled Buns

*A*t your next dinner party, surprise and delight your family and guests with a lovely basket of freshly baked buns that contain one of two different savory fillings. A basic yeast dough made with all-purpose and rye flours is shaped into buns that are stuffed with either a tomato-basil filling or an herbed cottage-cheese-and-mushroom mixture. Since the dough requires only one rising, you can prepare and bake these buns while you're putting the finishing touches on the rest of the meal.

Dough

- 2 cups all-purpose flour plus extra for dusting
- 2 cups rye flour
- ½ packet dry yeast
- 1 teaspoon salt
- 1¼ cups whole milk, heated to lukewarm
- 3 tablespoons vegetable oil

Filling 1

- 5 mushrooms, cleaned and coarsely chopped
- ½ cup cottage cheese
- 2 tablespoons finely chopped fresh parsley
- Salt and pepper

Filling 2

- 8 cherry tomatoes
- 8 fresh basil leaves
- 8 pinches of dried oregano
- Salt

1. In large bowl, stir all-purpose flour, rye flour, dry yeast, and salt until well combined.

2. Add lukewarm milk and oil to dry ingredients; stir until dough holds together. Dough will be sticky.

3. Knead dough on lightly floured surface until smooth and elastic, adding flour if necessary; cover and let rise in warm, draft-free spot for 30 minutes.

4. Combine ingredients for each filling. Add salt and pepper to filling 1; salt filling 2 to taste.

5. Divide dough into 16 equal pieces. Stuff 8 pieces with filling 1; stuff the other 8 with filling 2. Moisten hands with water and form buns around filling.

6. Place buns on greased baking sheet. Brush with water; dust with flour. Bake in preheated 400°F oven for 20 minutes.

Makes 16 buns

Herbed Cheese Squares

As aromatic and satisfying as any home-baked yeast bread, these savory squares can be whipped up in a jiffy thanks to baking powder, which eliminates the need for rising. A dough of flour, baking powder, salt, marjoram, grated cheese, melted butter, and buttermilk is rolled out and cut into small squares. After just a few minutes in the oven, they are ready to be served on an hors d'oeuvres tray or in a basket at dinner.

What You'll Need

- 2 cups whole-wheat flour, plus extra for dusting
- 1 teaspoon baking powder
- ½ teaspoon salt
- 3 teaspoons dried marjoram
- 3 ounces grated aged Gouda cheese
- 3 tablespoons unsalted butter, melted & cooled, plus extra for greasing
- ⅔ cup buttermilk
- ¼ cup walnuts
-   Rotary pastry cutter
-   Whole milk for brushing

1. Sift flour, baking powder and salt into large mixing bowl. Stir in marjoram and grated Gouda cheese.

2. Add melted butter and buttermilk to bowl; stir to combine. On lightly floured surface, knead to form dough.

3. Preheat oven to 425°F. Grease baking sheet; set aside. Chop walnuts; set aside.

4. Shape dough into ball. On lightly floured work surface, roll out dough to 8×10-inch rectangle, ⅓ inch thick.

5. With rotary pastry cutter or sharp thin-bladed knife, carefully cut dough into 2-inch squares.

6. Place squares about 1 inch apart on prepared baking sheet. Brush with milk, sprinkle with walnuts and bake 15 minutes. Serve warm.

Makes about 20 (2-inch) squares

Scented Hot Pad

*T*his spice-filled pad not only protects your tabletop from heat marks but also emits a warm, spicy scent every time a hot dish or pot is placed on it. Made from two pieces of heavy fabric, the pad is large enough to place under a casserole or kettle. The hot pad is tied like a quilt to keep the layer of aromatic spices evenly distributed.

What You'll Need

- **2 (8"×10") pieces heavy fabric & matching thread**
- **Scissors & straight pins**
- **4" decorative cord for hanger**
- **Sewing machine**
- **About ½ pound assorted aromatic spices, such as cinnamon sticks, star anise, & cloves**
- **1 skein darning cotton & darning needle**

— Tips & Techniques —

Heavy cloth such as denim or upholstery fabric works best, but if you wish to use thinner fabrics, line the pad with cotton batting. Tying the pad at intervals keeps the filling evenly distributed. If you like, mark the fabric with tailor's chalk before tying. The ties shown are made by taking a stitch from the top, leaving a long tail, and then reversing the needle's motion to make a second stitch, leaving a long loop. The loops are trimmed, then the threads are double knotted on both sides of the pad.

1. Place two fabric pieces right sides together; pin. Form cord into loop and pin at corner, so raw ends fall into seam.

2. Stitch all around, leaving ½" seam allowance and stitching loop into seam. Leave a 3" opening.

3. Turn fabric right side out. Break cinnamon sticks into pieces. Insert all spices through opening.

4. After filling pad, turn raw edges of opening under. Sew opening closed with small hand stitches.

5. Thread darning needle with darning cotton. Make diagonal rows of tying stitches (see Tips), working evenly across pad.

6. Cut loops; tie tight double knots in all stitches. Trim threads evenly. Hang pad from loop on hook near stove, so it is close at hand.

Nutty Bacon Rolls

These fragrant, savory rolls are a tasty accompaniment to a multicourse meal. Crispy bacon, sautéed onions, spicy olives and crunchy sunflower seeds are kneaded into a tangy yeast dough that is shaped into rounds. The mixture is then flattened into disks and baked until golden brown. These rolls combine complementary flavors and textures, which allow them to go well with almost any main dish. Serve them in a napkin-lined basket and garnish with sprigs of fresh thyme.

What You'll Need

- 1 (2-ounce) package fresh yeast
- Pinch of sugar
- 1 cup lukewarm milk
- 3½ cups all-purpose flour
- ½ teaspoon salt
- 7 tablespoons unsalted butter, at room temperature
- 1 egg
- 6 ounces smoked bacon, cubed
- 1 onion, chopped
- ⅓ cup pitted Kalamata olives
- 1 tablespoon dried thyme
- ½ cup sunflower seeds
- 1 tablespoon heavy cream

1. Mix yeast, sugar and milk. Mix flour, salt, butter and egg. Combine mixtures; knead until smooth. Let rise.

2. Partially cook bacon in skillet over medium heat. Add onion; cook until onion is golden and bacon is crisp.

3. Coarsely chop olives and crumble thyme. Add to bacon-onion mixture; stir to combine.

4. Knead bacon-onion mixture and ⅓ cup sunflower seeds into dough. Cut into 14 equal pieces; shape into rounds.

5. Place rounds on parchment-lined baking sheet 2 inches apart and flatten into disks. Brush with cream.

6. With small sharp knife, make shallow crosses in tops of rolls. Sprinkle with remaining sunflower seeds. Bake in preheated 400°F oven for 15 to 20 minutes, or until browned.
Makes 14 rolls

Oven-Fresh Herbed Bagels

*O*nce strictly an ethnic specialty, bagels now appear on almost any table for any meal, but especially at breakfast or brunch. Made from a basic yeast-and-egg dough, these tasty bagels are flavored with sautéed herbs and minced shallot. The dough is formed into balls that are flattened, cut to look like doughnuts, and then baked until golden. Traditionally served with cream cheese and smoked salmon, these bagels go well with almost any spread or sandwich filling.

What You'll Need

- 3 cups flour
- 1 ounce fresh yeast, crumbled, or 2 (¼-ounce) envelopes dry yeast
- 1 teaspoon sugar
- About 1 cup warm milk
- Several sprigs each parsley, basil, and oregano
- 1 shallot
- 10 tablespoons unsalted butter
- ½ teaspoon salt
- 1 egg
- 1 egg yolk, lightly beaten

1. In bowl, make well in flour. Pour in yeast, sugar and milk; knead until blended. Cover, place in warm spot and let rise 10 minutes.

2. Wash and pat dry herbs; remove and discard stems. Finely chop leaves. Peel and mince shallot.

3. Heat butter in skillet over medium heat. Add herbs and shallot; sauté until soft. Let cool.

4. Add herb-shallot mixture, salt and egg to dough; knead until smooth. Cover, set aside in warm spot and let rise 1 hour.

5. Shape dough into balls, place on baking sheet, and flatten. Cover with damp towel; let rise 10 minutes. Preheat oven to 350°F.

6. Cut centers out with cordial or shot glass. Brush with egg yolk. Bake about 30 minutes. Serve warm. Freeze in airtight plastic bag up to 2 months.
Makes 10 (4-inch) bagels

Papier-Mâché Pumpkin Bowl

Make a lightweight replica of a pumpkin's distinctive form using papier-mâché. All you need is newspaper, wheat paste, paint, and a well-formed pumpkin. Depending upon the size of the pumpkin you select, in no time you can make a buffet-size bread basket, a medium-size fruit bowl, or a miniature candy dish.

What You'll Need

- Newspaper
- Plastic bowl
- Wheat paste or wallpaper adhesive
- Large mixing container & wooden spoon
- Pumpkin
- Oil or petroleum jelly
- Utility knife, scissors, hot-glue gun, & glue sticks
- Acrylic paints: orange & yellow
- Paintbrushes

— Tips & Techniques —

Wash the pumpkin, pat dry, and, with a sharp knife, cut off the stem. Mix the wheat paste, a powdered adhesive sold in art supply stores, according to the package directions. Papier-mâché will air-dry completely in 24 hours or in 2 to 3 hours in the oven at its lowest temperature setting. To straighten the bowl rim, trim it with scissors; to smooth the seam, apply an additional layer of papier-mâché.

1. Tear newspaper into small pieces. In plastic bowl, mix wheat paste and water to form thin liquid.

2. Place newspaper pieces and paste in large container; stir mass with spoon until paper is saturated.

3. Place pumpkin stem side down; coat with oil. Overlap soaked paper to cover pumpkin to desired height.

4. Let papier-mâché dry completely. Make two cuts, top to bottom, halving bowl; remove halves from pumpkin.

5. Hot-glue halves together. Trim and smooth rim and seam as directed. Apply two coats of orange paint; let dry.

6. Apply yellow paint to highlight curves. If desired, paint inside of bowl. Let dry completely before using.

Mushroom-Filled Logs

V ersatile, easy to prepare and tasty—what more could a hostess ask for? Made from store-bought frozen puff pastry that is thawed, rolled out, and cut into large rectangles, these crispy, rolled pockets are stuffed with a spicy mixture of sautéed mushrooms, bacon and onion. These logs are perfect for an impromptu cocktail party, a luncheon buffet or a prelude to a formal dinner. Served warm or cold, arranged on a tray or in a cloth-lined basket, they are guaranteed to please your guests.

What You'll Need

- 1 package (17¼ ounces) frozen puff pastry
- 8 ounces bacon
- 1 medium onion
- 2 tablespoons butter
- ½ cup drained, canned whole mushrooms, finely chopped
- 1 tablespoon tomato paste
- ½ teaspoon salt
- ½ teaspoon freshly ground pepper
- 1 tablespoon flour, sifted
- 2 egg yolks, lightly beaten

1. Thaw puff pastry. On lightly floured surface roll into an 18-inch square to cut. Using chef's knife, chop bacon. Peel and chop onion.

2. Sauté bacon in skillet over medium heat until fat is rendered. Add onion and sauté until golden.

3. Add butter and mushrooms; stir to combine. Season with tomato paste, salt, and pepper. Stir in flour. Let cool.

4. Prepare logs: Spoon cooled filling in strip down length of each pastry rectangle to within ¾ inch from top and bottom.

5. Brush edges of pastry with water. Fold sides over filling to form logs. Press edges together to seal.

6. Place logs on foil-lined baking sheet. Prick dough with fork and brush with egg yolk. Bake on foil-lined baking sheet on middle of preheated 350°F oven for 30 minutes.

Makes 12 pastries

Red Pepper Muffins

*C*all it muffin madness, but it's easy to understand why these tasty little quick breads have achieved such popularity. Sweet or savory, fast and easy to whip up, muffins can be served at any time of day either by themselves or alongside almost any food. These savory red pepper muffins are an excellent accompaniment to salads and omelets, soups and stews, or any lightly seasoned meat or poultry.

What You'll Need

- 1 **egg**
- 1 **cup whole milk**
- 4 **tablespoons (½ stick) unsalted butter, melted & cooled**
- 1 **small sweet red pepper**
- 3 **ounces Emmentaler cheese**
- 1½ **cups all-purpose flour**
- ½ **teaspoon salt**
- 1 **tablespoon baking powder**
- **Pinch of chili powder**
- 12 **paper muffin-tin liners**

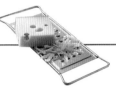

1. In medium mixing bowl, whisk egg, milk and butter until well blended and smooth.

2. Wash pepper; pat dry. Core, seed and cut pepper into small cubes. Coarsely grate cheese.

3. In separate bowl, combine flour, salt, baking powder and chili powder. Preheat oven to 400°F.

4. Pour egg-milk mixture into dry ingredients; stir until just combined. Stir in red pepper cubes.

5. Place paper liners in muffin-tins or grease only bottoms of tins. Divide batter equally among tins, filling each no more than two-thirds full.

6. Bake muffins for 25 to 30 minutes, until golden and tops split. Remove from tins as directed; let cool at least 1 hour before serving.

Makes 1 dozen muffins

Cloth Bottle Bags

Freshly squeezed orange juice or apple juice makes a great get-well gift, especially when it comes in bottles nestled in cheerful calico bags. The fabrics coordinate with felt cutouts of apples or oranges, framed on white cotton squares with bright rickrack trim. These easy-to-sew cloth bags can be adapted to fit bottles of any size, making it easy to wrap homemade oils, vinegars, liqueurs, or any other bottled offering. Pretty ribbon bows tie the bags closed.

—Tips & Techniques—

To sew the bags: Fold the fabric in half lengthwise with right sides together. Sew the long edges together with a ½" seam and turn the seam to the middle of the back of the tube. Sew the tube shut along the bottom edge with a ½" seam. Turn the bag right side out and turn the top 4"-6" to the inside, depending on the height of the bottle. If you need a pattern to draw the fruit, use a glass or a cookie cutter about 2" in diameter.

1. Cut calico fabric to size for bags. Cut white cotton in half to make two 4" squares.

2. Draw and cut from felt: one orange, one light green apple, two dark green leaves, one dark green stem, and one brown stem.

3. Glue orange, leaf, and green stem to one white square; glue apple, leaf, and brown stem to remaining square.

4. Pin squares to fabric, positioning equidistantly from sides and 5" from bottom edge; sew with zigzag stitch.

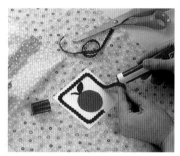

5. For a decorative frame, glue red braid or rickrack all around white squares about ¼" from edge.

6. Sew bags as directed in Tips, turning down 4"-6" at top. Insert juice-filled bottles into bags. Tie bags with matching ribbon bows.

Crispy Pizza Balls

*S*picy, crispy and fragrant, these fresh-from-the-oven tidbits are simply irresistible. The mouth-watering aromas of thyme, tomatoes and salami promise a delicious taste treat—and they deliver. Served by themselves with a glass of wine, as an afternoon snack, a prelude to an Italian meal or part of a buffet, they are sure crowd-pleasers. Easy to prepare and ready in a jiffy, these flavor-packed morsels are also the perfect solution for an impromptu gathering.

- 2 cups all-purpose flour
- ¾ ounce fresh yeast
- ½ teaspoon salt
- Pinch of sugar
- 1 small tomato
- 1½ ounces salami
- 2 ounces Gouda or Parmesan cheese
- 1 teaspoon each of dried thyme and oregano
- 2 tablespoons olive oil

1. Crumble yeast into flour, add 3 tablespoons water and stir to combine. Let mixture stand 10 minutes.

4. On lightly floured surface, knead diced ingredients, cheese and herbs into dough. Let stand 10 minutes.

2. Add salt, sugar and ¼ cup warm water; stir until dough forms. Knead dough and let stand 15 minutes.

5. Line baking pan with foil or parchment. Divide dough into 10 pieces of equal size; shape each piece into ball.

3. On cutting board, with sharp knife, peel, core and dice tomato; dice salami. Grate cheese.

6. Place pizza balls on baking pan; let rest 10 minutes. Brush each ball with olive oil and bake on middle rack of preheated 400°F oven for about 10 minutes, or until golden.
Makes 10 pizza balls

Ham Croissants

Stuffed croissants are more than elegant breakfast food; with a salad, they make a satisfying lunch. You can also pack them up for a potluck, picnic or tailgate party. Rather than puff pastry or yeast dough, these croissants are made with an easy-to-prepare quark and butter dough and filled with a rich mixture of smoked ham, créme fraîche, and scallions. Each dough triangle is rolled up and shaped into the traditional crescent, brushed with glaze, sprinkled with caraway seeds and baked until golden.

What You'll Need

Dough

2¾ cups all-purpose flour, plus extra for work surface

2 teaspoons baking powder

½ teaspoon salt

8 ounces quark, drained in fine-mesh sieve for 30 minutes

½ pound (2 sticks) butter, well chilled & cut into pieces

Filling

3 scallions

8 ounces smoked ham

4-6 leaves fresh sage

¼ cup crème fraîche

Salt & freshly ground pepper

Glaze

1 egg yolk lightly beaten with 4 tablespoons milk

2 tablespoons caraway seeds

1. Combine all dough ingredients; knead into smooth dough. Shape into ball; cover and chill for 15 minutes.

2. Wash scallions and pat dry; cut into thin rings. Cut ham and sage into thin strips.

3. Mix crème fraîche, ham, sage and scallions. Season to taste with salt and pepper. Preheat oven to 400°F.

4. Halve dough. On floured surface, roll out each half to 12-inch diameter circle; cut each into 8 triangles.

5. Spoon filling in center of triangle base; fold edge over filling and roll up triangle. Press tip gently; bend ends in to form crescent. Place on parchment-lined baking sheet.

6. Brush with yolk mixture; sprinkle with caraway seeds. Bake for 25-30 minutes, until golden.

Makes 16 croissants

Fresh Herb Wreath

*H*erbs bring tasty nuances and tempting aromas to any dish. This makes a wreath of fresh herbs the perfect decoration for any kitchen! Everyone in the house can enjoy its natural appearance and fragrance, and the cooks can break off the vitamin- and mineral-rich seasonings to use while creating their recipes.

—Tips & Techniques—

You can make a wreath from just one herb or combine several to enjoy the contrasts in color and texture. Fresh material will shrink as it dries, so make the bunches very full to compensate. If you use soft herbs, such as parsley, dill, or basil, you'll have to dry the wreath flat for a week or two to prevent them from drooping. Cut the stems of the herbs short, so the bunches will easily follow the curve of the frame when wired.

1. With scissors, cut herbs to 3" sprigs. Wire them together in separate bunches by type.

2. Wrap loose end of floral wire around base twice to anchor it. Twist loose end onto spooled wire to secure.

3. Lay bunch of rosemary on base; wrap with wire. Place next bunch over stems of previous one; wire to base.

4. Continue with sage, then attach bunches of other herbs, arranging them evenly around base.

5. Lift first bunch, place stems of last bunch underneath, and secure with wire. Twist wire on back and cut.

6. Attach a wire hanging loop if desired. Tie on wire-edged ribbon; make bow and form ends into rippling streamers.

Aromatic Thyme Rolls

T he dough for these golden herbed yeast rolls is prepared in the usual manner. However, after the dough has completed its final rising, the rolls are cooked in a skillet in hot butter, rather than baked on a pan in the oven. This is a common bread-making technique used in the Middle East. It intensifies the flavor and aroma of the chopped fresh thyme and produces a satisfying chewy texture. Serve the rolls warm to accompany vegetable, meat, poultry and fish dishes.

What You'll Need

- ⅓ cup whole milk
- 1¾ cups all-purpose flour
- 1 teaspoon salt
- 1 teaspoon sugar
- 1½ tablespoons fresh yeast, crumbled
- 1 egg
- 3 tablespoons chopped fresh thyme, or 2 tablespoons dried thyme, crumbled
- Vegetable oil for greasing baking pan
- 3 tablespoons unsalted butter

1. Heat milk until lukewarm. Sift flour into mixing bowl. Add salt to flour; whisk to combine.

2. Stir sugar and yeast into warm milk. Pour milk mixture into flour; stir to combine. Cover and let rise 20 minutes.

3. Add egg to dough and knead until well blended. Cover and let rise again, about 40 minutes.

4. Add thyme and knead into dough until evenly distributed. Cut dough into 16 equal pieces; form into balls.

5. Place balls on greased baking sheet. Press to flatten slightly; cover and let rise another 20 minutes.

6. Heat butter in skillet over medium heat. Add rolls and cook 4-5 minutes per side. Transfer to paper towels to drain. Serve warm.

Makes 16 round rolls

Braided Easter Rolls

T he baking of special breads is an integral part of Easter observances. To make these holiday rolls, a simple yeast dough is separated into fifteen equal portions that are rolled into strands, braided and shaped into circles. The braided circles are partially baked, then brushed with egg yolk and sprinkled with fresh chervil before they are returned to the oven until golden. Embellished with dyed hard-cooked eggs, these rolls will add a festive touch to your table.

What You'll Need

- 5 cups all-purpose flour
- 2⅓ cups rye flour
- 4 teaspoons salt
- 1 teaspoon sugar
- 2 envelopes active dry yeast
- 3 cups water
- 1 egg yolk, lightly beaten
- ⅔ cup finely chopped fresh chervil
- 5 dyed hard-cooked eggs (optional)

1. In large bowl, combine flours, salt, sugar and yeast. Add water; knead until smooth, soft dough is formed.

2. Cover dough with damp kitchen towel; let rise for 1 hour in a warm, draft free spot. Once dough is doubled in size knead briefly on floured surface. Cut into 5 equal-size pieces.

3. Cut each piece into thirds; roll into strands about ¾ inch thick and 12 inches long. Line baking pan with parchment.

4. Braid 3 strands; form into circle, pinching ends. Place on prepared pan.

5. Preheat oven to 400°F. Let braids rise for 15 minutes covered with a damp towel and placed in warm spot. Bake on middle rack of oven for 20 minutes.

6. Brush with egg yolk, sprinkle with chervil, and bake another 10 minutes. Let cool. Garnish with dyed hard-cooked eggs, if desired.

Makes 5 rolls

Tasty Herbal Blends

People all over the world custom-blend dried herbs to use in teas and other infusions for their beneficial properties. Try this soothing combination of lemon balm, thyme, sage, peppermint, and chamomile to help ward off a cold, relieve some of the discomfort of the flu, or just to relax. To ensure potency, dry fresh herbs picked from your garden and mix them into a blend of herbal TLC.

— Tips & Techniques —

Use only untreated herbs for tea and pick most before they bloom. The best time is late morning when the dew has dried but the heat of the day has not wilted the plants or dispersed the oils. Harvest the whole stem, not just the leaves, and always pick more than you think you'll need. Air-drying the herbs will take a few days to 2 weeks. You can also quick-dry herbs by putting them on a paper towel in the microwave on High for 1 minute. Dried herbs will keep for about a year in airtight tins or jars. For a cup of tea, steep 1 tablespoon of dried herbs for 5 to 10 minutes.

1. Make single-herb bouquets of sprigs of lemon balm, thyme, sage, and peppermint. Tie each with string.

2. Hang bouquets upside down in a dry, airy spot out of direct sunlight. Let dry until they feel crisp.

3. Spread out chamomile blossoms on clean tea towel and leave them until dried, about 1 week.

4. Remove leaves from stems of dried herbs. Sort leaves by type into individual bowls or containers.

5. In bowl, combine 2 parts chamomile blossoms, 1 part each lemon balm, sage, and peppermint, and ½ part thyme.

6. Put herbal mixture into jars or tins with airtight lids.

Pull-Apart Cheese Bread

Freshly baked bread is a guaranteed crowd pleaser, especially when it comes in the form of a crinkled pull-apart loaf stuffed with sautéed onion and four cheeses: Gorgonzola, mascarpone, Gouda and Cheddar. It is made with packaged refrigerated roll dough, each piece of which is rolled into an oval, stuffed with one of two cheese mixtures, then folded and pressed to encase the filling. The pockets are then arranged in a tube pan and baked until golden brown.

What You'll Need

2 ounces Cheddar cheese

3½ ounces mascarpone/Gorgonzola torta

1 small onion

1 tablespoon plus 1 teaspoon unsalted butter

3½ ounces aged Gouda

Salt & freshly ground pepper

3 packages refrigerated premade roll dough

1 (10-inch) tube pan, greased

5 tablespoons heavy cream

3 tablespoons poppy seeds

1. Grate Cheddar into mixing bowl. Add torta; stir with fork until blended.

2. Peel and finely chop onion. Sauté in butter over medium heat until transparent; set aside to cool.

3. Grate Gouda. Add Gouda to cooled onion; stir until blended. Season with salt and pepper to taste.

4. Separate dough; roll each piece into oval. Fill half with Cheddar mixture; half with Gouda mixture.

5. Fold in long sides of ovals to meet, then press edges together. Arrange in greased tube pan, pressing together the edges of adjacent pockets.

6. Brush top with cream; sprinkle evenly with poppy seeds. Bake as package label directs. Serve warm.

Makes 1 (10-inch) loaf

Rustic Herb Flatbread

I t's the simple things that make life pleasant, and that is certainly true when it comes to home-baked bread, especially one as tasty as this rustic flatbread. After its first rising, a simple yeast dough flavored with rosemary and thyme is divided in two, shaped into flat oblongs and left to rise once more. Before the loaves are baked, they are brushed with a glaze and sprinkled with more herbs. Crusty and fragrant, these loaves will go well with anything from a simple repast to a full-course dinner.

3½ cups all-purpose flour, plus extra for work surface

1 teaspoon salt

1 teaspoon sugar

1 (0.6-ounce) cube fresh yeast

1 cup warm water

1½ tablespoons dried rosemary, divided

2½ tablespoons dried thyme, divided

1 tablespoon olive oil, plus extra for greasing baking sheet

1 egg white

1. Sift flour, salt and sugar into large bowl. In small bowl, stir yeast and water until yeast dissolves.

2. Sprinkle 1 tablespoon rosemary and 2 tablespoons thyme over flour mixture. Add yeast mixture; knead to form dough.

3. Cover dough with damp towel; let rise in warm spot for 30 minutes. Preheat oven to 425°F.

4. Coat hands with olive oil and knead dough briefly on clean, dry, lightly floured surface. Divide dough in half; shape into flat oblongs. Oil large baking sheet.

5. Place flatbreads on baking sheet. Mix 1 tablespoon olive oil, egg white and 1 tablespoon water; brush on breads.

6. Sprinkle breads with remaining herbs; let rise for 20 minutes. Bake in preheated oven for about 30 minutes.

Makes 2 loaves

Decorative Herb Pot

Growing a variety of compatible herbs in a pretty planter is both practical and pleasurable, because fresh herbs impart the most flavor, and they are fragrant and attractive. The potted herbs shown include dill, chives, thyme, summer savory, and oregano, but try making your own selection. With a ready supply of fresh herbs, don't hesitate to make herbal oils, vinegars, butters, garnishes, teas, sachets, and beauty treatments, all of which make wonderful gifts.

What You'll Need

4–5 different compatible herbs

Trowel & cultivator

Terra-cotta planter, 10" in diameter

Drainage materials: stones, pot shards, or gravel

Potting soil: high-quality, sterilized, & well-draining

Wide decorative ribbon, 1 yard

— Tips & Techniques —

Herbs that are planted together must be compatible and require the same maintenance. For instance, bergamot and mints need more water than other herbs do. Dill, thyme, oregano, marjoram, parsley, chives, and savory grow well together. Fast-growing herbs, like tarragon, fennel, lovage, peppermint, and lemon balm should have their own pot. Lavender, bay leaf, sage, rosemary, and basil should be planted singly. For optimal growth, place the herb pot outdoors regularly to spend some time in the sun and fresh air, otherwise the herbs will become straggly after a few weeks.

1. Purchase pots of healthy compatible herbs (see Tips) about equal in growth size. Gather tools, such as a trowel and cultivator.

2. Water herbs well; leave 1 to 2 hours. Place drainage materials in bottom of planter. Remove herbs from pots.

3. Fill pot two-thirds full with potting soil. Place tall-growing herbs in back of planter and bushy ones in front.

4. With trowel, carefully fill in around plants with more soil. Press down firmly and add more soil as necessary.

5. Water planter well. Cover surface of soil with small stones to keep soil moist and add a decorative touch.

6. To give planter as gift, wrap a decorative bow around it, identify herbs, and give maintenance instructions.

Lighthouse Gift-Wrap Tube

Many kinds of gifts—wine, candles, rolled artwork and maps, and the Painted Bottles for Olive Oil on page 40—are best wrapped in a strong cardboard tube. An easy and imaginative way to decorate the tube is to cover it with lightweight white cardboard and apply colored adhesive tape to create a glowing lighthouse.

What You'll Need

- 2 lids for tube ends
- 1 sturdy cardboard tube
- Adhesive tapes in desired widths: black, red, yellow
- Scissors, pencil, & compass
- Lightweight cardboard or construction paper: large white sheet & small red piece
- Double-sided adhesive tape

— Tips & Techniques —

Purchase or recycle a cardboard tube large enough to fit your gift. Both ends must be covered, either with the plastic inserts that come with the tube or with substitutes fashioned from wooden cheese boxes, margarine container lids, etc. Cut the tube to the length you need, then cut lightweight cardboard to wrap around it with an inch or so overlap. For decorating, art stores sell masking tape in the colors used here, but electrical tapes will also work.

1. Attach lid to tube with vertical strips of tape. Wrap black tape horizontally around base.

2. Wrap white cardboard around tube above base; attach along overlapped edge with double-sided adhesive tape.

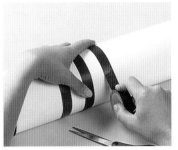

3. Mark location of red stripes. At markings, wrap tube with red tape, overlapping edges and pressing down.

4. Wrap top of tube with wide strip of yellow tape for windows. Cut and attach yellow rectangles for lower windows.

5. With black tape, frame windows at top, bottom, and sides. Apply black tape for lighthouse door.

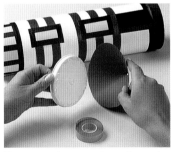

6. For roof, cut red cardboard circle 2" larger than lid; cut slit from edge to center. Overlap and glue edges to create point. Glue roof to lid; place on tube.

Heart-Shaped Spice Bread

There are many occasions during the year for the giving of hearts, so why not express your feelings by baking a heart-shaped bread that not only tastes great but is also healthy and nourishing? Made of hearty yeast dough, it is flavored with chopped fresh herbs and seasoned with spicy caraway and fennel seeds. Presented in a lovely basket lined with the fresh herbs used inside the bread or nestled in a colorful cloth napkin, it makes a wonderful hostess gift baked "from the heart."

What You'll Need

- 2 cups rye flour
- 2 cups whole-wheat flour
- 1½ ounces fresh yeast
- ½ teaspoon sugar
- 2 cups lukewarm water, divided
- 1 bunch fresh dill
- 1 bunch fresh parsley
- 2 bunches fresh chives
- 1 teaspoon each of salt, caraway seeds, and fennel seeds
- Margarine for greasing pan
- 4 tablespoons margarine, melted

1. Sift rye and wheat flour into large bowl; stir to combine. Make depression in middle and crumble yeast into it.

2. Add sugar and ½ cup lukewarm water to yeast; stir until dough forms. Cover and let rise in a warm spot for 20 minutes.

3. Wash and trim herbs; chop finely. Add herbs, salt, remaining water, caraway and fennel seeds to dough.

4. With floured hands, knead dough until all ingredients have been incorporated and dough is smooth and shiny.

5. Grease heart-shaped pan. Fit dough into pan, cover and let rise in warm spot 30 minutes. Preheat oven to 425°F.

6. Carve concentric hearts into surface with a sharp, wet knife; brush with margarine. Bake 35 minutes with a water-filled oven proof bowl on the bottom of the oven. Cool on wire rack.
Makes 1 (10-inch) loaf

Stamped Wooden Wine Box

A good bottle of wine is always a welcome gift, especially when it's presented in a hand-stamped wooden wine box. The geometric pattern of squares and diamonds in appealing red and green is achieved with old-fashioned, easy-to-make potato stamps. The box is so attractive that, after the wine has been used, the lucky recipient will be able to put it to use storing photographs, letters, audiocassettes, or other collectibles.

— Tips & Techniques —

Wooden wine boxes can be found at liquor stores or craft shops. To create this pattern, you need three simple templates: a square, a small diamond, and a large diamond with an open center. Draw them on heavy paper, and cut out. To make the potato stamps, apply the templates to the cut side of the potato and slice away the excess potato flesh. You can stamp two to three motifs before refreshing the paint.

1. Cut the potatoes crosswise; for smaller stamps, cut into quarters. With paper towels, pat dry the cut surfaces.

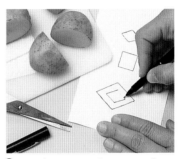

2. On heavyweight paper, draw all three templates (see Tips), cut out, and position onto cut potato surfaces.

3. Cut potatoes, following outlines of templates. Scoop away potato from interior of large diamond.

4. In a bowl for each color, mix 1 tablespoon each of paint and water. Stamp red squares on box edges and large diamonds in center. Let dry.

5. Using green paint, stamp small diamonds within large red diamonds and in open areas. Let dry.

6. Cushion interior of box with excelsior. Place wine bottle inside box. Replace lid.

Sourdough Rye Bread

Nothing can top homemade bread for flavor, texture and aroma. And this beautiful crusty sourdough loaf may be the reason why. A soft yeast dough made with rye and whole-wheat flours, sourdough starter and caraway is given several risings before it is shaped into balls that are left to rise in traditional coiled bread bowls that give the loaves an Old-World look. This flavorful bread is excellent with strong cheeses, cold cuts and hearty soups and stews.

What You'll Need

- 1½ cups whole-wheat flour
- 8½ cups rye flour, divided
- 3½ cups warm water
- ½ cup sourdough starter
- 1½ ounces fresh yeast mixed with 2½ tablespoons water
- 1 heaping tablespoon salt
- 2 tablespoons coarsely ground caraway seeds
- 2 large round or oval ceramic or stoneware bowls

1. In large mixing bowl, combine whole-wheat flour, 3½ cups rye flour, warm water, and starter.

2. Cover and let rise 24 hours. Add yeast mixture; whisk until blended. Cover and let rise for 30 minutes.

3. Add remaining rye flour, salt and caraway seeds; knead to form sticky dough. Cover and let rise for 3 hours.

4. Dust ceramic bowls liberally with flour; set aside. On well-floured surface, shape dough into 2 balls. Place dough in bowls; cover and let rise for 1 hour. Tip dough balls over onto floured baking sheet. Preheat oven to 450°F and place a pan of water on the bottom rack.

5. Let dough rise for 5 minutes, then place in bottom third of oven. Reduce oven temperature to 350°F and bake for 60 to 70 minutes. Turn oven off, sprinkle loaves with water and let rest in oven for 5 to 10 minutes. Transfer to wire racks to crisp.

Makes 2 (1½-pound) loaves

Cotton Bread Bags

Instead of using an old-fashioned bread basket, serve your morning baguette or keep your home-baked loaf warm in a bright fabric bread bag. Made of washable cotton, lined with contrasting fabric, and tied with drawstring bows, these cheery bags can be machine-sewn in a matter of minutes. Not only are they unique and attractive servers on a breakfast, brunch, or tea table, but they also make a perfect wrapping for a gift of homemade bread.

What You'll Need

Scissors, tape measure, iron, sewing machine, thread, & safety pin

For baguette bag:

1 strip plain cotton fabric, 36" long

2 pieces checked cotton fabric, 8"×20"

2 pieces striped cotton fabric, 8"×5"

For bread loaf bag:

1 strip plain cotton fabric, 36" long

2 pieces checked cotton fabric, 9½"×13"

2 pieces striped cotton fabric, 9½"×5"

— *Tips & Techniques* —

To make the tunnel for the tie, measure 2½" from the top of the fabric rectangle and, using tailor's chalk or basting stitches, mark the top of the tunnel; then, measure down 1" more and mark the bottom of the tunnel. Leave openings at the seams to run the tie through. For each tie, make one long strip or cut it in half and make two strips, one for each side of the bag.

1. To make tie, trim fabric strip to 1½" wide. If necessary, piece together remnants to make 1½"×36" strip.

2. Press ¼" fold on each long side, then fold strip in half; press and topstitch. Slip stitch ends.

3. To make bags, sew checked fabric to striped fabric with right sides together, top edges aligned. Press seam open.

4. Right sides together, sew pieces along sides and bottom with ½" seam, leaving 1" openings for tie (see Tips).

5. Fold striped lining inside bag; press. Mark tunnel for tie (see Tips). Stitch along marks through both layers.

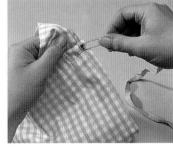

6. Attach safety pin to tie; thread through tunnel. Insert bread, pull tie to gather bag, and tie ends in a bow.

Crust and Crumb   49

Good Luck Bread

These aromatic loaves of yeast bread are shaped like horseshoes, traditional symbols of good luck. The dough, which contains two kinds of flour, is flavored with caraway seeds, cardamom and coriander, spices favored by Old World bakers. After two risings, the dough is shaped, brushed with milk and marked with caraway seed "nails" before baking. Bring a loaf or two to your next housewarming or serve them at a congratulatory dinner.

1. Sift both flours and salt into large mixing bowl. Combine yeast and warm water; stir until blended.

2. Add yeast mixture to flour; knead until dough is formed. Cover and set aside to rise 50 minutes.

3. Add ground caraway seeds, coriander and cardamom to dough; knead vigorously until blended. Cover dough and set aside to rise 50 minutes. Preheat oven to 425°F.

4. Line baking sheet with parchment. Knead dough and divide into thirds.

5. Form each third into horseshoe, making ends thinner than middle. Flatten slightly on prepared baking sheet.

6. Brush with milk. Make 4 small depressions in each horseshoe "leg" and fill with caraway seeds. Bake 15 to 30 minutes, until golden brown and sounds hollow when tapped.
Makes 3 small loaves

Stoneware Spice Bread

omemade bread is always a welcome component of any picnic, party or dinner. Although it requires a bit of extra effort and planning to accommodate two risings, this flavorful, chewy loaf will quickly disappear from the table. Made from all-purpose and rye flour, sourdough starter and buttermilk, the bread also contains honey, caraway, coriander and anise for a uniquely spicy flavor. Bake bread in a moistened stoneware pan to develop an extra-crispy crust.

What You'll Need

- 4 cups all-purpose flour
- 2¾ cups rye flour
- 2 envelopes active dry yeast
- 2 teaspoons ground caraway
- ½ teaspoon each of ground coriander and anise
- 4 teaspoons salt
- ⅔ cup sourdough starter
- 1 teaspoon honey
- 2 cups lukewarm water
- 1¼ cups buttermilk
- 2 teaspoons caraway seeds

1. Combine flours in large mixing bowl. Whisk in yeast.

2. Combine ground caraway, coriander, anise, salt and flour mixture. Stir in starter. Combine honey and lukewarm water. Add to buttermilk; stir until blended.

3. Add buttermilk mixture to flour, kneading until dough is smooth and no longer sticky. Cover with damp kitchen towel, place in warm spot and let rise until doubled in size, about 1 hour.

4. Knead dough a few turns; shape into oval. Place in moistened unglazed stoneware pan, cover and let rise 10 minutes.

5. Using thin-bladed sharp knife, cut crisscross lines in dough. Brush with water, sprinkle with caraway seeds and bake on middle rack of preheated 425°F oven 1 hour or until loaf sounds hollow when bottom is tapped.

Makes 1 (3½-pound) loaf

Stamped Fruit & Vegetable Labels

L abel jars with colorful stamped images of your homemade fruits and vegetables to brighten your pantry or to make charming hostess gifts. The filled glass jar is dressed up by a circle of fabric tied around the lid with a bow of yarn or twine. Then the fruit or vegetable, created on white foam, is stamped onto a label that will easily identify your canned treats.

What You'll Need

White foam for stamping

Fine-tip permanent black pen

Scissors

Craft glue, hot-glue gun & glue sticks

Wooden squares

Acrylic paints & paintbrush

Wooden beads, ½" in diameter

Heavy paper or adhesive labels

— Tips & Techniques —

The stamps are cut from a rubbery, firm foam made for decorative stamping, which is sold at art and craft supply stores. The smooth finish makes full contact with the stamping surface and does not soak up the paint you apply. The foam stamps are attached to thin wooden squares that you can buy precut in craft stores. Stamp onto white self-adhesive labels if you wish to press the finished label directly onto the container. Use edging scissors to make fancy edges on your labels.

1. Draw outline of fruit or vegetable onto foam with permanent ink. Image will be reversed when stamped.

2. Using scissors, carefully cut out each shape. Shapes must fit onto wooden squares with a little space all around.

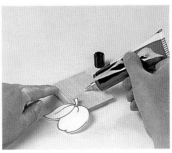

3. With craft glue (for flat fit), glue shaped foam to center of wooden square and press firmly to adhere.

4. Turn over stamp and hot-glue wooden bead to center of wooden square to create a handle.

5. On foam side of stamp, paint motif with lightly loaded paintbrush, leaving interior design lines and highlights bare.

6. Press stamp firmly onto cut paper or labels. Add details with brush as necessary; let dry. Attach label.

Crust and Crumb   55

Braided Poppy Seed Bread

N o longer just a Jewish Sabbath tradition, this beautiful, delicately flavored yeast bread has become a favorite with many families for serving at holidays and special dinners. The required four risings are time-consuming but well worth the moist, tender texture. Delicious fresh from the oven, this bread also makes fabulous sandwiches and French toast. Two loaves handsomely presented in a napkin-lined basket is a thoughtful hostess gift.

What You'll Need

- 5¼ cups all-purpose flour, plus extra for kneading
- ½ envelope yeast
- 1 teaspoon sugar
- 1¼ cups lukewarm water
- ½ pound baking potatoes, cooked in their skins and cooled
- 2 eggs
- 1½ teaspoons salt
- 3 tablespoons vegetable oil
- 1 egg white, lightly beaten
- 4 tablespoons poppy seeds or sesame seeds

1. Sift flour into large bowl; make depression in center. In large measuring cup, mix yeast, sugar and water.

2. Pour yeast mixture into depression; stir until combined. Sprinkle with some flour; let dough rise 20 minutes.

3. Peel potatoes; discard skins. Put potatoes through ricer. Add potatoes, eggs, salt and oil to dough.

4. Knead dough until smooth; cover with damp kitchen towel and let rise 1 hour. Knead; cover and let rise 45 minutes.

5. Knead dough briefly; cut into 6 equal pieces. On lightly floured surface, roll each piece into 16-inch long rope.

6. Form 2 braids; cover and let rise 20 minutes. Brush with egg white and sprinkle with poppy seeds. Bake braids on separate parchment-lined baking pans in preheated 375°F oven 35 to 40 minutes, until golden brown.
Makes 2 loaves

Rustic Multigrain Bread

Nothing beats the aroma and taste of just-baked bread, and this crusty, round loaf is no exception. The bread is formed with a nutritious mixture of six grains and sunflower seeds combined with tangy sourdough starter, yeast, barley malt and salt. After two risings, the dough is sprinkled with rolled oats, then baked until golden. Time consuming but easy to prepare, this tasty loaf makes extra-crunchy morning toast or bread for a hearty sandwich.

What You'll Need

- 2²⁄₃ cups rye flour
- ²⁄₃ cup sourdough starter
- 2¹⁄₂ cups water, divided
- ³⁄₄ cup each rolled oats, cracked wheat, and wheat germ
- ¹⁄₂ cup each millet & sunflower seeds
- 1 cup whole-wheat flour
- 3 teaspoons salt
- 1 tablespoon barley malt
- 2 envelopes active dry yeast
- 2 tablespoons whole milk
- 2 tablespoons rolled oats for sprinkling

1. Combine rye flour, starter, and 1 cup water; stir. Let rise for 15 hours.

2. Carefully measure out and assemble all remaining ingredients and equipment.

3. Add 1¹⁄₂ cups water and remaining ingredients except milk and 2 tablespoons oats into flour mixture, knead on lightly floured surface until stiff but pliable and no longer sticky, adding small amounts of flour or water as necessary.

4. Let rise 2 hours, then knead dough briefly. Shape and place on greased and floured baking pan. Let rise another 2 hours.

5. With sharp oil-dipped knife, make 1-inch deep crisscross cuts in top of loaf. Brush with milk.

6. Top loaf with oats; bake in middle of preheated 400°F oven for about 1 hour, or until loaf sounds hollow when tapped on bottom. Cool before serving.
Makes 1 (2¹⁄₂-pound) loaf

New Year's Bread

Every culture has its special New Year's tradition to invoke the health and happiness we wish for ourselves and for our loved ones. In Greece, the new year is celebrated with a rich anise and orange rind-flavored yeast bread that is stuffed with a foil-wrapped coin before it is sprinkled with sesame seeds, garnished with blanched almonds and popped into the oven. As is Greek custom, the bread is served with wine to toast the person who gets the coin and, with it, a year of good luck.

What You'll Need

- 3½ cups all-purpose flour plus extra for kneading
- 1 cube fresh yeast
- 6 tablespoons warm water
- ½ cup sugar, divided
- 6½ tablespoons butter, melted and cooled
- 3 eggs
- ½ teaspoon salt
- 1 teaspoon ground anise
- Grated rind of 1 orange
- 10½-inch springform pan
- 1 shiny new coin, wrapped in foil
- 1 egg yolk, lightly beaten
- 3 tablespoons sesame seeds
- Blanched almonds for garnish (optional)

1. Sift flour into large mixing bowl. Using large spoon, make deep depression in center.

2. Crumble yeast into cup. Stir in warm water and 1 teaspoon sugar; pour into flour. Cover; set aside 30 minutes.

3. Add remaining sugar, butter, eggs, salt, anise and orange rind to bowl; stir to combine.

4. Knead dough until smooth and no longer sticky. Cover and let rise 45 minutes. Grease springform pan.

5. Fit dough into pan. Press coin inside dough. Brush with egg yolk; sprinkle with sesame seeds.

6. Garnish loaf with almonds. Let rise 15 minutes. Bake on middle rack of preheated 350°F oven for 35 minutes until bottom sounds hollow when tapped.

Makes 1 (10½-inch) round

Painted Bottles for Olive Oil

Flavorful and healthful olive oil is most economically purchased in large quantities, which can be decanted into smaller containers for convenient use or gift-giving. Wine bottles painted with olive branches are perfect for this purpose. The motifs are traced and transferred to the bottles with carbon paper, then painted with glass paints. The paint hardens in the oven to a durable finish that can withstand washing.

What You'll Need

Tracing paper & carbon paper

Pencil, scissors, & cellophane tape

2 clean wine bottles & new corks

1 tube black oven-hardening glass or tile outliner (liquid leading)

Oven-hardening glass or tile paints: dark blue, green, brown, white

Soft paintbrushes

—Tips & Techniques—

For maximum durability, use glass or tile paints and outliner that can be hardened in the oven. Follow the instructions that come with each product regarding drying and hardening. Before painting, rub alcohol on the outside of the bottle where the motif will be. When covering solid areas, dot on the paint to avoid the stripes that brushing can create. Prevent runs by not overloading the paintbrush. Wet paint can be removed with a cotton swab, and dried errors can be scraped off with a razor blade or craft knife. If using recycled bottles, remove all labels before painting. Sterilize the bottles before filling them.

1. From book or other source, trace attractive olive branch and olive motif onto tracing paper.

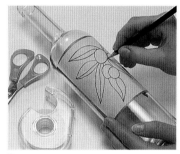

2. Tape carbon paper, carbon side down, on bottle with tracing paper over it. Pressing hard, redraw outlines.

3. With glass outliner, draw over design lines. Following manufacturer's instructions, let dry.

4. Paint dark blue olives on first bottle. Leave narrow arcs unpainted to add highlights and dimension.

5. Paint leaves green on both bottles, following curves of motif.

6. Mix green and brown paints to make olive green. Paint olives on second bottle; let dry; paint white highlights on both bottles. Let bottles dry upright, then bake, following manufacturer's instructions.

English Tea Cake

Tea and its service have a long history, but it's the goodies that go with it, like this festive tea cake, that hold our attention. Rum-soaked raisins and currants, liqueur-laced candied cherries, as well as candied citrus rinds, are added to a batter flavored with vanilla and lemon extracts and the fruits' soaking liquids. To keep the baked loaf sweet and moist, brush it with a simple lemon-flavored glaze. Perfect for afternoon tea or coffee, this lovely cake is rich enough to serve for dessert.

What You'll Need

- 1 **cup raisins**
- ½ **cup currants**
- 5 **tablespoons dark rum**
- ⅓ **cup candied cherries**
- 4 **tablespoons cherry liqueur**
- 1 **cup (2 sticks) unsalted butter**
- ¾ **cup sugar**
- 1 **teaspoon vanilla extract**
- ¼ **teaspoon lemon extract**
-   **Pinch of salt**
- 4 **eggs**
- 2¾ **cups all-purpose flour**
- 1½ **teaspoons baking powder**
- ¼ **cup each candied lemon & orange rind**
- 1 **(9-inch) loaf pan**
- 1 **cup confectioners' sugar**
- 2-3 **tablespoons lemon juice**

1. Combine raisins and currants in bowl; add rum. Place cherries in bowl; add liqueur. Steep fruit overnight.

2. Cream butter and sugar. Beat in vanilla and lemon extracts and salt. Beat in eggs, 1 at a time, until blended.

3. Drain fruit through sieve, reserving liquids; set fruits aside. Add liquids to butter mixture; beat until blended.

4. Sift flour and baking powder into butter mixture; beat just until blended. Batter will be thick.

5. Halve drained cherries. Mince candied lemon and orange rinds. Fold all fruits into batter; pour into greased 9-inch loaf pan.

6. Bake in a preheated 350°F oven for 70-80 minutes, until tester comes out clean. Partially cool. Mix confectioners' sugar and lemon juice; brush over warm loaf.

Makes 1 (9-inch) loaf

A Tea Drinker's Delight

This decorative tin lined with fabric and overflowing with an assortment of teas and accessories is truly a tea drinker's delight. Beautiful airtight containers keep the teas fresh. Sticks of crystallized sugar sweeten a cup of tea with just a swirl. A measuring spoon and a bamboo strainer make brewing loose-leaf tea a snap. There's even a bag of cookies and a jar of sweet vanilla rum to add a little spice.

What You'll Need

- Decorative tin or box & lining fabric
- Assortment of teas, containers, & bags
- Crystallized sugar on sticks
- Measuring teaspoon & bamboo strainer
- Glass jar with tight-fitting lid
- Sugar candy, vanilla bean, & rum
- Labels, marking pen, & glue
- Tea cookies & paper bag
- Accessories, such as tea infuser, hourglass timer, & tea bag holder
- Cellophane, ribbons, & raffia

— Tips & Techniques —

For the tea chest, select a pretty reusable container and a heavy luxurious fabric, such as satin or velvet, for the lining. Teas are available in a wide variety of traditional as well as new and exotic blends. Pick an assortment of teas you think your recipient will like, perhaps one from each of the three general categories of green (unfermented), oolong (semifermented), and black (fermented). Generally, 1 heaping teaspoon is used per 6-ounce cup, plus 1 for the pot. Be sure to include any instructions that come with the teas.

1. Loosely line inside of decorative tin with pretty fabric. Fill containers and bags with varieties of tea; seal tightly.

2. Wrap crystallized sugar sticks with cellophane. Tie teaspoon measure and bamboo strainer together with ribbon.

3. Wash and dry glass jar. Place sugar candy and vanilla bean in jar, then fill with rum. Seal jar tightly.

4. Decorate labels and name items, giving instructions for use. Glue to or hang from containers, bags, and jar.

5. Pack everything attractively in the tin, placing heavy items in center and tucking light accessories around edges.

6. Place tea cookies in pretty paper bag. Decorate bag with raffia bow. Present cookie bag with tea tin.

Apple Puff Pastries

Nothing brings back pleasant childhood memories like the aroma of fresh-baked apples wafting from the kitchen. This apple recipe is sure to satisfy all ages. Filled with rum-soaked nuts and raisins, enveloped in a delicate pastry, and presented on a lovely plate, it is a sophisticated twist on an otherwise timeless treat. Whether served warm or cold, with or without whipped cream, this apple is sure to please everyone's taste buds.

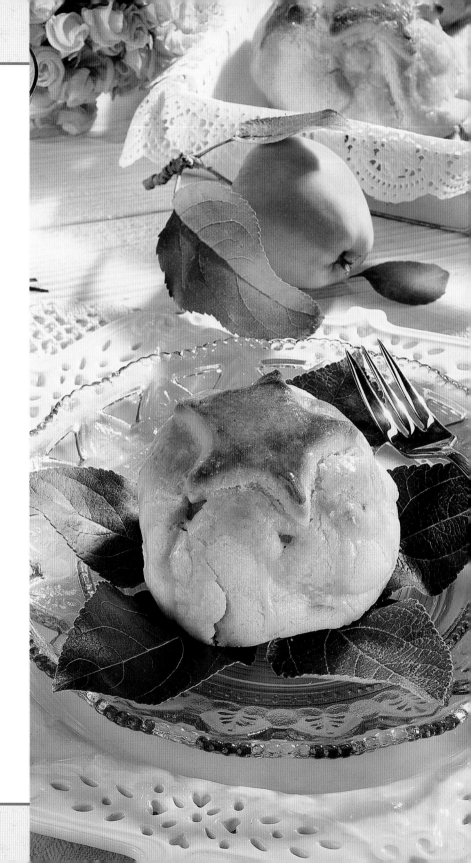

What You'll Need

Dough

- 2 cups all-purpose flour
- 9 tablespoons butter
- $\frac{1}{3}$ cup sugar
- Pinch of salt
- Grated peel of $\frac{1}{2}$ lemon
- 1 egg

Filling

- 8 small tart apples
- $\frac{1}{4}$ cup raisins
- $\frac{1}{4}$ cup chopped walnuts
- 2 tablespoons ground hazelnuts
- 3 tablespoons light honey
- 2 tablespoons dark rum
- 1 egg yolk, lightly beaten

1. Combine dough ingredients; knead just until holds together. Shape into disk. Cover; chill. Wash, pat dry and peel apples. Remove cores and discard.

2. For filling combine raisins and nuts in a small bowl. Add honey and rum; mix well and set aside.

3. Roll out dough on lightly floured surface. Using rim of bowl and small pastry wheel, cut out rounds for apples making sure to cut enough dough to cover each apple.

4. Place apple in center of dough; fill core with raisin-nut mixture. Enclose in dough. Cut stars from remaining dough scraps. Place star on top of each apple.

5. Place apples on a lined baking pan. Brush with egg yolk and bake for 30 minutes in preheated 375°F oven.

Makes 8 servings

Blueberry Tarts

Almost as American as apple pie, blueberry tarts are a true summertime treat. Juicy and bursting with flavor, individual tarts are sure to delight the palate. Inside the crispy shell is a filling of sweet blueberries, creamy mascarpone cheese and chopped hazelnuts. Of course, the tarts are best when made with fresh blueberries, but frozen berries work well, too. You'll want to make these tarts often when berry season is in full swing, varying the selection of summer berries.

What You'll Need

Dough

- 1 cup flour
- Pinch of salt
- 1/4 cup sugar
- 7 tablespoons butter, cut into pieces;
- 1 egg

Filling

- 1/4 cup chopped hazelnuts
- 1 pint blueberries
- 8 ounces mascarpone cheese
- 3/4 cup sugar
- 1 teaspoon vanilla extract
- 1 egg yolk
- Grated peel of 1 lemon
- 1 tablespoon confectioners' sugar

1. Combine flour, salt, sugar and butter. Make indentation at top and add egg. Knead together until smooth; if too dry, add 1 or 2 tablespoons of milk.

2. Wrap dough in plastic wrap and refrigerate for 1 hour. Then, on floured surface, roll out dough to 1/8 inch thick.

3. Cut dough circles 2 inches larger than diameter of tart pans; gently press into bottoms of pans. Line with foil and fill with weights, rice or dry beans. Place pans on a baking sheet and bake in preheated 350°F oven until golden, about 15 minutes.

4. Remove foil with weights; cool shells for 10 minutes. Sprinkle chopped hazelnuts on bottoms, then fill generously with blueberries.

5. Beat mascarpone, sugar, vanilla, egg yolk and lemon peel until smooth; spoon into tarts. Bake 35 minutes at 350°F.

6. Let blueberry tarts cool. Sprinkle confectioners' sugar through sieve over individual tarts.

Makes 8 individual tarts

Fudge Almond Brownies

*C*hocolate brownies have been a popular treat for generations. Everyone has their favorite version: rich and fudgy or light and cakelike, frosted or plain, and with or without nuts, candy chips, swirls of chocolate, or other flavorings. Brownies are a delectable dessert, perfect with milk, coffee or tea and, when decorated with colored icing and candles, they make terrific birthday cakes. This fudgy version features three popular additions: coffee to add a mocha flavor, a rich chocolate frosting and delicious almonds.

What You'll Need

Batter

- **6 ounces semisweet chocolate**
- **¼ cup (4 tablespoons) butter, plus extra to grease pan**
- **1 teaspoon instant espresso powder**
- **2 tablespoons whole milk**
- **¾ cup brown sugar**
- **¼ cup granulated sugar**
- **1 teaspoon vanilla**
- **⅔ cup all-purpose flour**
- **1 teaspoon baking powder**
- **⅛ teaspoon salt**
- **2 eggs**
- **¼ cup chopped almonds**

Topping

- **¾ cup prepared chocolate frosting**
- **2 tablespoons strong brewed coffee, cooled**
- **¼ cup sliced almonds**

1. Melt chocolate and ¼ cup butter over low heat. Stir in instant espresso, milk, brown and granulated sugars and vanilla.

2. Into bowl, sift together flour, baking powder and salt; whisk thoroughly to combine.

3. Transfer chocolate mixture to large bowl; stir in eggs. Add flour mixture and chopped almonds; stir until smooth.

4. Spread dough evenly in greased 9×9-inch baking pan. Bake 40 minutes in 350°F oven. Let cool in pan.

5. Transfer prepared frosting to bowl and add cooled brewed coffee. Mix until well blended.

6. Spread frosting over brownies; sprinkle sliced almonds over top, while frosting is moist. Cut into squares.
Makes 16 brownie squares

Holiday Stollen

Whatever country Christmas is celebrated in, there are traditional baked goods to be enjoyed. In Germany, stollen is THE holiday baked good. A rich fruit- and nut-filled yeast bread, with chopped almonds, almond extract, orange zest, cinnamon, nutmeg and cardamom, all kneaded into a buttery yeast dough. After it is baked, the stollen is brushed with melted butter and dusted with sugar for a festive finish, then set aside to mellow.

What You'll Need

- 6 cups all-purpose flour
- 2 ounces fresh yeast
- 1½ cups warm milk
- 2 eggs
- 1¼ cups granulated sugar, divided
- Pinch of salt
- 2 cups (4 sticks) unsalted butter, at room temperature, cut into pieces, divided
- ⅔ cup finely chopped blanched almonds
- 4 drops almond extract
- 2 teaspoons vanilla extract
- 2 teaspoons grated orange rind
- 1 teaspoon cinnamon
- Generous pinch each cardamom and nutmeg
- 2 tablespoons confectioners' sugar

1. In large bowl, make well in flour with fist. Crumble yeast into milk; add to flour. Mix; let rise 20 minutes.

2. Combine eggs, ¾ cup granulated sugar and salt. Add to dough; knead until incorporated. Let rise 30 minutes.

3. Add 1½ cups butter and remaining ingredients, except sugars, to dough; knead to combine. Let rise 15 minutes in a warm, draft-free spot.

4. Halve dough; shape into oval loaves. Place on parchment-lined baking sheets. Let rise 15 minutes.

5. Bake stollen 50 to 60 minutes in preheated 400°F oven. Mix remaining ½ cup granulated sugar with confectioners' sugar.

6. Let stollen cool. Melt remaining ½ cup butter. Brush cooled loaves with butter and sprinkle evenly with mixed sugars; pat gently to adhere.

Makes 2 loaves

Miniature Message Breads

*A*t your next party,
surprise your family
and guests by serving them
crispy, savory appetizers with
a secret or two tucked inside.
Like Chinese fortune cookies,
these tasty nibbles contain a
symbol of significance: a small
piece of paper with a good-
luck heart is considered a
ticket for happiness and love.
You can also enclose a special
event ticket, a party invitation,
or perhaps a little love note.
Whatever message you
enclose, it's sure to get the
conversation flowing.

What You'll Need

- 1²⁄₃ **cups all-purpose flour**
- 1 **teaspoon baking powder**
- 1 **teaspoon salt**
- ¹⁄₃ **cup freshly grated Parmesan cheese**
- ¹⁄₂ **cup butter, melted**
- ¹⁄₄ **cup water**
- 1 **egg yolk**
- 1 **tablespoon heavy cream**
- 1 **tablespoon sesame or poppy seeds**

— Tips & Techniques —

Before you start making the bread, design the happiness tickets: Cut 20 (2"×3") rectangles of parchment paper. With a nontoxic felt pen, draw a heart in the middle of each one and add a personal message if you wish. Start mixing the dough with a handheld kneading device, then finish by hand. Place the dough in a warm, draft-free spot; let set for 1 hour. If time is limited, use store-bought, frozen puff pastry.

1. Mix flour, baking powder, salt and cheese. Heat butter and water; add to bowl. Beat until blended.

2. Place dough in warm spot for 1 hour. On floured surface, roll dough into ¹⁄₂"-thick rectangle.

3. Using pastry wheel or sharp knife and rolling pin or ruler, cut out 20 (3"×4") rectangles.

4. Place each fortune ticket (see Tips) atop one dough rectangle; roll into cylinder. Twist ends.

5. Beat egg yolk and cream; brush rollups with mixture. Sprinkle with sesame or poppy seeds. Grease a baking pan.

6. Bake rollups in preheated 375°F oven for about 25 minutes. Cool on rack; tie ends with ribbons.

Yield: This recipe makes approximately 20 appetizers

Poppy Seed Coffee Cake

*O*ne of life's simple pleasures, homemade coffee cake can lift your spirits, boost your energy, and satisfy your sweet tooth all at the same time. This delightful version calls for a simple yeast dough flavored with lemon rind and cinnamon that is topped with a crunchy mixture of ground poppy seeds, biscotti, sugar, pudding mix, raisins, milk and butter, then covered with streusel and baked. This fragrant cake is wonderful with steaming coffee and makes a welcome treat for a friend or hostess.

What You'll Need

Dough and streusel

2⅔ cups all-purpose flour, divided

½ cup sugar, divided

2 egg yolks

½ cup (1 stick) unsalted butter, at room temperature

1 teaspoon grated lemon rind

6 tablespoons warm milk

1 (0.6-ounce) cube fresh yeast, crumbled

½ teaspoon cinnamon

Topping

8 ounces poppy seeds

2 ounces plain biscotti or zweiback

⅓ cup sugar

2 tablespoons vanilla pudding mix

Pinch of salt

½ cup seedless raisins, soaked in hot water, until plump, and drained

1½ cups whole milk

3 tablespoons unsalted butter

1. Combine 1⅓ cups flour, 2 tablespoons sugar, 1 yolk, 2 tablespoons butter, lemon rind, milk and yeast; knead to form dough. Cover and let rise.

2. With hands, combine remaining flour, sugar, yolk, butter and cinnamon; cover and chill.

3. For topping, finely grind poppy seeds and biscotti in food processor or blender. Combine with sugar, pudding mix, salt and raisins.

4. In nonreactive pan, bring milk and butter to boil; add poppy seed mixture. Cook, over medium-low heat, whisking constantly, for 2 minutes; cool.

5. Roll dough; fit into 10-inch round springform pan. Spread with poppy seed mixture; let rise for 15 minutes.

6. Crumble streusel evenly over cake; bake in preheated 350°F oven for 35-40 minutes, until toothpick inserted in center comes out clean.

Makes 1 (10-inch) coffee cake

Hot Cross Buns

A traditional Good Friday offering, these subtly sweet, light yeast buns are great to serve with coffee or tea any time. Currants and candied orange rind are mixed into a yeast dough flavored with ground cloves and cinnamon that is shaped into buns. A flour-butter dough is rolled and cut into strips that are crisscrossed on the buns. After baking, the buns are glazed with milk and sugar, then baked a few minutes more. Serve them warm with homemade jam and sweet butter.

What You'll Need

3½ cups flour

⅓ cup sugar

½ teaspoon cinnamon

¼ teaspoon each ground cloves and nutmeg

Salt

¾ cup dried currants

⅓ cup diced candied orange rind

3½ tablespoons unsalted butter, melted and cooled

1 egg

1 (0.6-ounce) cube fresh yeast

¾ cup warm milk

Crosses

½ cup flour

2 tablespoons cold butter

1 tablespoon water

Glaze

2 tablespoons sugar mixed with 2 tablespoons whole milk and boiled until sugar has dissolved

1. In large bowl, mix flour, sugar, spices, salt, currants and candied orange. Add butter and egg; stir to combine.

2. Whisk yeast and milk until blended; add to flour mixture. Knead gently to form pliable dough for buns.

3. Cover and let dough rise for 45 minutes. For crosses, knead flour, butter and water to form dough; chill. Punch down bun dough and knead on lightly floured surface until smooth and elastic.

4. Divide and shape into 12 equal-sized buns; let rise, covered, on parchment-lined baking sheet 30 minutes.

5. Roll dough for crosses into ½-inch wide strips; cut into 3 inch lengths and crisscross 2 lengths on top of each bun.

6. Bake buns in preheated 400°F oven for 15 minutes. Glaze, then bake 3 minutes. Cool slightly on wire rack; serve warm.

Makes 12 buns

Raisin-Ricotta Tartlets

*P*uffed and golden, these pretty tartlets look like they came straight from the bakery. But you can make them in a jiffy right in your own kitchen. Store-bought puff pastry is cut into rounds, then nestled into the cups of a muffin pan. The cups are filled with a creamy mixture of sweetened ricotta, eggs and raisins that is flavored with lemon and Marsala wine and baked to perfection. For an elegant finish to a formal dinner, serve the tartlets warm with a decanter of Marsala.

What You'll Need

- 1 (17¼-ounce) package frozen-puff pastry, thawed
- 2 lemons
- ¼ cup Marsala wine
- 8 ounces ricotta
- 1 whole egg plus 2 egg yolks
- 6 tablespoons sugar
- ½ cup raisins

1. Place individual sheets of thawed puff pastry flat on lightly floured surface. Cut out 6 rounds from each sheet of dough with 3½-inch biscuit cutter. Pack tightly into greased muffin pan cups.

2. Wash lemons and pat dry; finely grate rind of both and set aside. Measure out ¼ cup Marsala wine.

3. Combine ricotta, egg and egg yolks, sugar, lemon zest and Marsala; whisk until smooth and creamy.

4. Combine raisins and enough hot water to cover; "plump" 5 minutes. Drain and add to filling.

5. With large spoon or ladle, divide cheese filling equally among pastry-lined muffin pan cups.

6. Bake in preheated 350°F oven for 25 minutes. Loosen tartlets with thin-bladed knife before removing from pan. Serve warm.

Makes 12 tartlets

Sunflower & Fruit Basket

*N*o flower is more cheerful and evocative of its namesake than the sunflower. Here, a bunch of medium-size sunflowers mingles beautifully with clusters of ripe grapes in a pretty basket to mark the bittersweet end of summer. Grapevines, goldenrod, and Saint-John's-wort—or any other late-summer wildflower you prefer—fill out this rustic table arrangement or gift basket. To complete the picture, the basket handle is wrapped with ribbon in an appealing sunflower print.

—Tips & Techniques—

For wrapping the basket handle, choose decorative ribbon that is printed on both sides, as they both will show after the bows are tied. Wrap the handle tightly, then glue the ends of the ribbon to the handle. To prepare the flowers, remove the leaves from the flower stems, then hold the stems underwater and cut them on an angle to the appropriate length. Insert the stems as deep as possible into the floral foam to anchor them securely. Check foam daily and add water as needed.

1. With sharp knife, cut floral foam to fit bowl; round off corners and sides on angle. Soak foam in water 15 minutes.

2. Reserving enough for two bows, wrap ribbon around basket handle (see Tips). Tie on ribbon at each end; make bows.

3. Place bowl with foam in basket. Bend 8" lengths of floral wire in half. Use to attach bunches of grapes to foam.

4. Insert grape leaves evenly around foam. Insert grapevines into foam, allowing them to trail over basket edges.

5. Cut sunflower stems on angle to length that does not extend beyond handle. Insert into center of foam.

6. Insert goldenrod into foam, hanging some flowers over sides of basket. Insert Saint-John's-wort with berries.

Apple & Cheese Scones

Usually sweet, fruity pastries served with jam also make excellent savories, and scones are no exception. These tender, crumbly biscuits are spiced with curry powder and contain freshly grated tart apple and Gouda cheese. The apple and cheese are kneaded into a butter-enriched dough, which is rolled out and cut into rounds that are baked for 15 minutes. Serve with a light lunch of soup or salad, or use them to add pizzazz to a fruit and cheese platter.

What You'll Need

- 1½ cups all-purpose flour plus extra for dusting
- 1 teaspoon baking powder
- 1-2 teaspoons mild curry powder, or to taste
- Pinch of salt
- 3½ tablespoons unsalted butter
- 1 medium tart apple, such as Granny Smith
- 5 ounces aged Gouda, grated (about 1 cup)

1. Sift flour and baking powder into mixing bowl. Add curry powder and salt; whisk to combine.

2. Cut butter into small pieces. Add to dry ingredients. By hand, knead into a crumbly dough.

3. Peel, halve and core apple; grate finely. Strain off apple juice. Add grated apple and cheese to dough.

4. In bowl, gently knead dough until ingredients are well combined and dough is smooth and firm.

5. On lightly floured surface, roll out dough to ¾-inch thickness. With a lightly floured 3-inch cutter cut out 12 scones.

6. Place scones on parchment-lined baking sheet. Bake in preheated 425°F oven for 12-15 minutes, until golden. Cool slightly and serve warm.
Makes about 1 dozen scones

Miniature Panettones

A popular Christmas tradition throughout Italy, panettone is a rich yeast bread that has become so well-known that it is now commercially produced and sold year-round in many countries. Made from an egg-enriched yeast dough, panettone is flavored with nutmeg and lemon zest and further embellished with candied orange and lemon peel, candied red cherries and raisins. Baked in small, round cylinders, these breads are perfect for a special holiday dessert or party favors.

What You'll Need

- 4 to 4½ cups all-purpose flour
- ½ cup sugar
- ½ package fresh yeast
- 1 cup warm milk
- ½ cup (1 stick) unsalted butter, melted
- 3 eggs
- 2 egg yolks
- Pinch of freshly grated nutmeg
- 1 teaspoon salt
- 1 teaspoon lemon zest
- ⅓ cup each candied lemon & orange peel
- 3 tablespoons diced candied cherries
- ¼ cup raisins
- Confectioners' sugar for dusting

1. Pour flour and sugar into large mixing bowl; whisk to combine. Make depression in center.

2. Crumble yeast into center; add milk. Mix into flour. Cover and let rise about 15 minutes.

3. Lightly whisk butter, eggs and yolks; add to flour. Add nutmeg, salt and zest; knead until well combined.

4. Cover dough; let rise until doubled. Meanwhile, grease molds. Knead candied fruit and raisins into dough.

5. Divide dough equally among 12 prepared molds; cover and let rise 25 minutes. Bake on middle rack of preheated 350°F oven for 35 minutes.

6. Cool breads on wire rack about 5 minutes, then remove from molds to cool completely. Dust with confectioners' sugar.
Makes 12 panettones

Candy Jar with Painted Decals

Turn a simple, old-fashioned candy jar into an artistic statement using glass paint cling-on designs. Just draw the outlines of the flowers and leaves with liquid leading on a plastic sheet, then fill in with colorful, nontoxic glass paints. When dry, press the painted designs, which are repositionable, onto the candy jar or any glass, mirror, or ceramic surface.

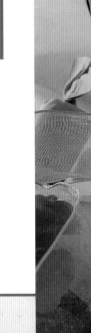

—— Tips & Techniques ——

You can buy glass paint (also called glass stain or window paint) as well as plastic or acetate sheets at craft stores, through mail order, or online. If the paint manufacturer's directions differ from these, follow theirs. Apply the glass paint thickly, up to the edge of the leading. You can use a toothpick to seal the paint against the black outline. Make sure the surface on which you will apply the painted decals is clean and free of grease or dust.

1. With felt-tip pen, draw outlines of flowers and leaves on paper. Include flower centers and leaf veins.

2. Lay plastic or acetate sheet over pattern, smooth out, and secure with masking tape.

3. Outline all lines of designs with a thin bead of black liquid leading. Let dry for 8 hours (or follow manufacturer's directions).

4. Thickly fill in segments of designs with paint. First flow around perimeter, then fill center. Let dry 24–48 hours.

5. When completely dry, carefully cut out designs using craft knife. Gently lift them off sheet.

6. Clean and dry jar. Arrange decals on jar; smooth out air bubbles and press firmly to attach. Wipe with damp cloth.

Double-Frosted Nut Cookies

Cookies aren't just for kids, as these elegant creations demonstrate. Roasted chopped hazelnuts add their delicate flavor to a butter-rich "short" dough spiked with cinnamon and brandy. The rolled dough is cut into small rounds and stars, baked until golden, then frosted twice: first with melted dark chocolate, then with narrow stripes of white chocolate, which are marbled for a lacy effect. Serve these treats with tea or coffee.

What You'll Need

Dough

- ½ **pound hazelnuts**
- 1½ **cups all-purpose flour**
- 1 **teaspoon baking powder**
- ½ **cup brown sugar**
- **Pinch salt**
- ¼ **teaspoon cinnamon**
- 4 **tablespoons brandy**
- 1 **egg**
- 7 **tablespoons butter, chilled**

Frosting

- ¼ **pound bittersweet chocolate**
- 2 **ounces white chocolate**
- **Wooden skewer**

1. For dough, roast hazelnuts, shaking pan, in hot, dry skillet until browned. Transfer to clean kitchen towel and gently rub to remove skins; finely grind. Combine nuts with remaining dough ingredients. Knead to form dough. Cover and chill 2 hours.

2. On lightly floured surface, roll out dough to ¼-inch thickness. Cut out circles and stars with cookie cutters.

3. Bake cookies on parchment-lined baking sheet on middle rack of preheated 350°F oven for 10 to 15 minutes.

4. For frosting, melt chocolates separately over simmering water. Working quickly so bittersweet chocolate remains warm, frost cookies.

5. Drizzle on narrow parallel lines of white chocolate. Draw skewer through chocolates in parallel perpendicular lines to create lacelike effect; skewer should draw through with little resistance if chocolates are still warm enough. Let set and store in airtight tin between layers of waxed paper to prevent cookies from sticking.

Makes 5 dozen cookies

Waffled Cookie Sandwiches

O ften it is the simple things we enjoy the most—like these crispy little cookie sandwiches. A sweet, rich cookie dough made with flour, ground almonds, sugar, egg and butter, and flavored with vanilla, grated orange peel and orange liqueur is cut into small rounds and baked in a waffle iron instead of the oven. Elegant enough for a formal tea or luncheon dessert, these nougat-filled mini sandwich cookies also make great after-school snacks.

What You'll Need

- ¾ cup all-purpose flour
- 1 cup finely ground almonds
- ¼ cup plus 2 tablespoons sugar
- ½ teaspoon baking powder
- Grated rind of 2 oranges
- 6 tablespoons orange liqueur (such as Cointreau) or orange juice, divided
- 2 teaspoons vanilla extract
- 1 egg
- 8 tablespoons (1 stick) cold butter, cut into pieces
- ¾ cup (3½ ounces) creamy nougat (such as Nutella®)
- Confectioners' sugar for sprinkling

1. On clean, dry work surface, mix flour, almonds, sugar, baking powder and orange rind.

2. Make depression in center; add 1 tablespoon orange liqueur, vanilla extract and egg.

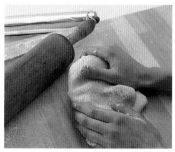

3. Distribute butter along rim; cut in with pastry blender. Knead into smooth dough; wrap in foil or plastic wrap and refrigerate 1 hour.

4. On lightly floured surface, roll out dough to ¼-inch thickness; cut out 2-inch rounds with cookie cutter. Reroll scraps and cut to make 40 rounds.

5. Bake rounds in preheated waffle iron on medium setting; spray with nonstick cooking spray or brush lightly with melted butter. Cool on wire rack. Mix nougat with remaining 5 tablespoons orange liqueur. Spread half the waffles with nougat mixture; top with plain waffles. Sprinkle liberally with confectioners' sugar.

Makes about 20 cookie sandwiches

Black-&-White Cookies

T he person who said "you can't please all the people all the time" forgot about cookies. These beautifully iced rounds are made from a simple dough dropped by heaping teaspoonfuls onto a baking sheet, then flattened and baked until golden. The rounds are cooled, then spread with both chocolate and lemon icing to form three enticing patterns. An easily made-ahead dessert, they are perfect to bring to a picnic, barbecue, or a July 4th extravaganza.

What You'll Need

Dough

9 tablespoons unsalted butter, at room temperature

1½ cups sugar

4 eggs

3 teaspoons vanilla extract

4 cups all-purpose flour

6 teaspoons baking powder

About 6 tablespoons whole milk plus extra for brushing

Icings

3½ ounces melted semisweet chocolate combined with 6 tablespoons heavy cream

3 cups sifted confectioners' sugar combined with 4-5 tablespoons fresh lemon juice

1. Cream butter. Gradually beat in sugar. Add eggs, one at a time, beating until each is incorporated. Add vanilla. Sift together flour and baking powder. Alternately stir in the dry ingredients and milk to egg mixture in 2 batches each, adding enough milk to form a sticky dough; stir to blend.

2. Drop heaping teaspoonfuls of dough at least 1½ inches apart onto parchment-lined baking sheets; flatten into rounds and bake in a preheated 350°F oven 15 to 20 minutes, or until golden. Brush cookies with milk after 10 minutes to brown them. Cool.

3. Using pastry brush or spatula, spread half of each of 9 cookies with chocolate icing, half with lemon icing.

4. Using wooden toothpick, drag chocolate icing into lemon icing, forming waves down center; let set.

5. Spread remaining cookies with lemon icing. Pipe chocolate in spiral and zigzag designs over icing; place iced cookies on wire racks until set.
Makes about 27 (3-inch) cookies

Cherry-Almond Biscotti

A delightful interpretation of an Italian classic, these golden cherry-studded biscuits are baked twice to achieve their crunchy texture. A traditional butter-enriched, flour-sugar-egg batter is flavored with vanilla and lemon extracts, then combined with marzipan and chopped amaretto-soaked cherries. Light in texture but rich in flavor, these biscotti are the perfect way to end a hearty meal.

What You'll Need

- 6 eggs
- 1⅓ cups confectioners' sugar
- 10 tablespoons unsalted butter, melted and cooled
- 1 teaspoon vanilla extract
- 2 drops lemon extract
- Pinch salt
- 2-3 tablespoons whole milk
- 7 ounces marzipan at room temperature
- 4 ounces amaretto-soaked maraschino cherries, drained
- 2 cups all-purpose flour, plus extra for dusting
- 1 teaspoon baking powder

1. Beat eggs and sugar in large mixing bowl until foamy. Beat in butter, vanilla and lemon extracts, salt and milk.

2. Cut marzipan into small pieces. Add to egg mixture; beat until completely incorporated. Preheat oven to 350°F.

3. Finely chop cherries; add to batter. Sift flour and baking powder into batter; stir until well combined.

4. Grease baking form or sheet; dust with flour. Pour batter into form or shape into oval and place on sheet.

5. Bake 55 to 60 minutes. Cool on wire rack. Cut crosswise into ½-inch-thick slices. Reduce oven temperature to 250°F.

6. On parchment-lined baking sheet, place slices flat. Bake for 20 minutes, or until crispy. Let cool; store in airtight container up to 4 weeks.

Makes about 2 dozen biscotti

Homemade Cookie Bags

*P*ackage your fresh-baked cookies in pretty, homemade gift bags. They are easy to create with wrapping paper, lightweight cardboard, and decorative cord or braid. You merely wrap the paper around a book, using it as a mold to create the shape. On the decorative paper covering the front cutout, you can write a name or add the motif of a special occasion.

—Tips & Techniques—

The beauty of this bag-making technique is its simplicity. The bag is essentially a wrapped book minus the book, with the top edge turned in rather than overlapped and glued. Make bags sized to fit any item by using an appropriate book or box as your mold. The size of the wrapping paper needed is: circumference of book + 1" X height + thickness of book + 1". You can attach the handles with the knots inside, outside, or on top. If you like, use materials of a coordinating color to outline the window and to make the handles.

1. Turn gift paper under 1" at top edge. Wrap book, with seam at back, creasing but not gluing folds.

2. Remove book and crease all folds again. Cut construction paper in shape of your choice for window pattern.

3. Draw diagonals on inside of front of bag to mark center. Position cutout pattern as desired and draw onto bag.

4. Cut out window. Glue decorative paper inside bag to cover window. Glue cord around window on front.

5. Align folded edge with top of book, and rewrap book. Glue long seam. Cut (or fold) and glue bottom edge.

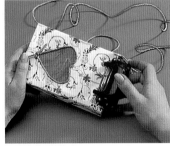

6. Punch two holes at top edge of front and back of bag. Tie cord handles to front and to back, knotting tightly.

Heavenly Amaretto Cookies

Italian almond macaroons, better known as amaretti, are seductively sweet cookies that can be served as a pleasant accompaniment to coffee, espresso, cappuccino or a light dessert. These baked delicacies are easy and inexpensive to make, and require only a few ingredients. Store them in a tin, so you will always have some on hand for a sweet treat for family and friends. But be prepared— these cookies won't last long!

What You'll Need

- ½ pound blanched almonds
- 4 drops bitter almond oil
- ¾ cup sugar
- 2 egg whites
- 1 tablespoon confectioners' sugar

1. Finely grind almonds in batches using hand grinder, blender or food processor.

2. Combine almonds with almond oil, sugar and lightly beaten egg whites. Knead mixture into firm dough.

3. With moistened hands, form dough into balls about 1 inch in diameter. You should have about 45 balls.

4. Place balls at least 1 inch apart on parchment-lined baking sheets. Use second baking sheet if needed.

5. Preheat oven to 250°F. Place baking sheet on bottom rack and bake for about 55 to 60 minutes.

6. Transfer baked cookies to wire rack. Dust cookies with confectioners' sugar while warm. Store in an airtight container for up to 1 month.
Makes about 45 cookies

Scottish Shortbread

*S*hort on flour but not flavor, these melt-in-your-mouth cookies contain an unusually high proportion of butter to flour, which is what gives them their unique taste and texture as well as their name. Unlike the more traditional shortbread recipes, this one is flavored with marzipan and ground vanilla bean. Traditional Scottish shortbread is baked in a round, patterned mold and then cut into wedges for serving. These simple cookies are perfect for afternoon tea or a bedtime snack.

What You'll Need

- **3 cups all-purpose flour**
- **½ cup sugar**
- **Pinch salt**
- **1 teaspoon ground vanilla bean**
- **3½ tablespoons marzipan**
- **1 cup (2 sticks) unsalted butter, chilled**

1. Sift flour into large mixing bowl. Add sugar, salt and ground vanilla bean; whisk to combine.

4. Cover dough; let rest 30 minutes. On lightly floured surface, roll out dough to ½-inch thickness.

2. Crumble marzipan; cut butter into small pieces. Add marzipan and butter to flour mixture.

5. Cut dough into 3×1-inch rectangles; using wooden skewer or fork, prick each cookie in several places.

3. Using your hands, knead mixture just until soft, pliable dough forms; do not overwork.

6. Place cookies 1-inch apart on parchment-lined cookie sheet; bake in preheated 300°F oven for 25 to 30 minutes, until golden. Store in an airtight container up to 2 weeks.
Makes about 5 dozen cookies

Pine Nut Cookies

Flavored with grated lemon rind and almond liqueur, these delicate pine nut morsels are crispy on the outside and chewy in the center. The cookies are traditionally served with coffee and tea, but they also make a satisfying after-school snack with milk or cocoa. With a dusting of confectioners' sugar, they look as if they came fresh from the bakery. Whip up an extra batch to pack in a decorative container for a lovely thank-you or hostess gift.

- 4 ounces pine nuts
- 1⅓ cups all-purpose flour
- ½ tablespoon baking powder
- 4 ounces (1 stick) unsalted butter
- ⅓ cup granulated sugar
- 1 egg
- 1 teaspoon grated lemon rind
- 2 tablespoons almond liqueur
- 2 tablespoons confectioners' sugar

1. Place pine nuts in clean, dry skillet over medium heat to toast them. Stir continuously until golden.

2. In food processor or with sharp knife, coarsely chop half of toasted pine nuts. Reserve remainder for garnish.

3. Mix flour and baking powder in large bowl. Add butter, granulated sugar, egg, lemon rind and liqueur; mix to blend. Chill 1 hour.

4. Using teaspoon, separate dough into walnut-size pieces; with moist hands, shape pieces into balls. Press 2 pine nuts into top of each ball; place 2 inches apart on parchment-lined baking sheet.

5. Bake cookies on middle rack of preheated 350°F oven for 20 minutes, until light brown.

6. On wire rack, sprinkle with confectioners' sugar while still hot; let cool before serving.
Makes about 30 cookies

A Bouquet of Roses & Cookies

The red rose is the classic symbol of love. A single rose whispers, "I care." A dozen roses say, "I love you." A bountiful bouquet of red roses and homemade, red-bowed, heart-shape cookies proclaim with joy, "I really, really love you"—a perfect Valentine's Day message. The delicious classic sugar cookies are simple and fun to make. You might invite your beloved to an intimate dinner for two, and let your heartfelt flower arrangement sing out your affection as the centerpiece.

Cookies

  2⅓ **cups sifted flour**

   ¾ **cup butter, softened**

   ½ **cup confectioners' sugar**

   1 **teaspoon vanilla extract**

   1 **egg**

     3" heart-shape cookie cutter

     Drinking straw

Bouquet

20" length of ¼"-wide red ribbon & long floral wire per cookie

24-36 red roses & stems of greenery

Raffia

— Tips & Techniques —

For an abundant bouquet, use 25 large roses or 35 small ones. Strip off the lower leaves, and cut each stem on a sharp angle. To extend the flowers' life, change the water in the vase daily and cut the stems 1" for better water absorption. The dough makes 3 dozen 3" cookies. Use a heart-shape cookie cutter of a size proportionate to the roses. Bake on parchment-lined cookie sheets in a preheated 350°F oven for 15 minutes.

1. On clean work surface, combine flour, butter, sugar, and vanilla extract. Make indentation in mixture and break egg into it.

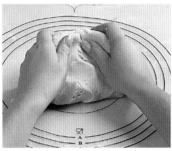

2. Knead everything together quickly. Wrap in plastic wrap and chill 1 hour, or until firm enough to roll.

3. On floured surface, roll out dough ⅛" thick. Cut hearts; place on prepared cookie sheet (see Tips). With straw, make a hole in each cookie. Bake.

4. Fold ribbon in half; knot to make loop. With loop in back, slide ends through hole and tie bow in front.

5. Roll one end of each length of wire around pencil to make loop. Hang cookies by ribbon loops from wires.

6. Tie roses and greenery into bouquet with raffia. Insert cookie wires and cut bottoms if necessary. Arrange in vase.

Pistachio-Orange Diamonds

These fancy diamond-shaped and iced sandwich cookies offer a truly unique combination of flavor, color and texture. Two layers of basic buttery shortbread dough are filled with a rich mixture of chopped pistachios, confectioners' sugar, coconut and grated orange rind and juice. They are then baked, cut into diamonds, and coated with orange-flavored icing. Pack them in a pretty box or tin and serve with coffee or tea for dessert.

What You'll Need

Dough

- 1¾ cups all-purpose flour
- 1 teaspoon baking powder
- 1 cup sifted confectioners' sugar
- 1 egg
- 10 tablespoons butter, cut into pieces

Filling

- ⅔ cup finely chopped pistachios
- 2½ tablespoons confectioners' sugar
- 2 tablespoons grated coconut
- Grated rind and juice of 1 orange

Glaze

- 2 tablespoons blood-orange juice
- 1 cup confectioners' sugar
- ⅓ cup candied orange rind cut into equal-size strips for garnish

1. Preheat oven to 400°F. For dough, combine flour, baking powder and 1 cup confectioners' sugar on work surface. Make well in center.

2. Add egg and butter. With hands, knead into firm dough; cover and refrigerate 1 hour.

3. For filling, in medium bowl mix chopped pistachios, 2½ tablespoons confectioners' sugar, grated coconut and orange rind. Add just enough orange juice to make mixture spreadable.

4. Halve dough; roll out each to 12×12-inch square. Transfer 1 half to parchment-lined baking pan; prick with fork.

5. Spread filling over dough. Top with second sheet; prick. Bake 20 minutes; cut into 2-inch diamonds while still hot. Cool.

6. For glaze, mix blood-orange juice and confectioners' sugar until smooth. Glaze cookies on wire racks over waxed paper; garnish with orange rind.

Makes about 32 sandwich cookies

Almond Cookies

For a delicious treat straight from the Middle East, try these melt-in-your-mouth almond butter cookies. After the dough is mixed and chilled, it is formed into a cylinder and sliced. Then the slices are gently rolled into balls, topped with a whole almond and baked. While still hot, the cookies are soaked in an exotic lemon-mint-rose water syrup. Excellent with coffee and tea, these traditional cookies also make a lovely gift.

What You'll Need

Dough

6 tablespoons unsalted butter, at room temperature

1 egg

Seeds from 1 vanilla bean

½ cup confectioners' sugar

Pinch salt

1⅓ cups sifted all-purpose flour

Garnish

25 whole blanched almonds

Syrup

1¼ cups sugar

¾ cup water

Juice from ½ lemon

1 teaspoon dried lemon peel

1 tablespoon crushed fresh mint leaves

2 tablespoons rose water

1. For dough combine butter, egg, vanilla bean seeds, confectioners' sugar and salt in bowl; stir until blended.

2. Add flour to mixture; knead to incorporate and form smooth dough. Cover with plastic wrap and refrigerate 2 hours.

3. Preheat oven to 375°F. On lightly floured work surface, roll dough into cylinder; cut crosswise into 25 equal pieces.

4. Roll each piece into ball; place at least 2 inches apart on greased baking sheet. Press 1 almond into each ball; bake 15 minutes at 375°F.

5. For syrup, bring sugar and water to boil. Add remaining ingredients; continue to boil until liquid clears.

6. Using a large slotted spoon, dip hot cookies into syrup until almost saturated. Transfer to wire racks to cool.

Makes about 25 cookies

Gilded Bowls

ilding, a magical decorative technique, transforms ordinary objects, like these bowls, into lustrous treasures. Shown to perfection against cobalt blue glass, the irregular patches of gold leaf create an opulent but casual look. Tape applied to the outside of the bowl serves as the pattern for the adhesive, which holds the gold leaf in place. Sealed against wear and tarnishing, these bowls will shine on any coffee, dining, or dressing table.

- Removable 1"-wide paper tape or masking tape
- 2 blue glass bowls, about 5½" in diameter
- Oil adhesive size & flat paintbrush
- 3–4 (5½") sheets composition gold leaf
- Soft cloth
- Soft-bristle paintbrush
- Clear nontoxic sealant & paintbrush

—Tips & Techniques—

Imitation gold leaf, known as composition leaf or Dutch metal, has made home gilding both practical and affordable. Composition leaf also comes in sheets of marbled designs with veins of red, green, or black. For the leaf to adhere, the surface of the bowls must be completely clean, dry, and free of oil. Follow the directions that come with the size, leaf, and sealant. Before you apply the leaf, the size must dry until barely tacky. Tap a knuckle on it; it's ready when it pulls the skin slightly and makes a snapping sound. Handle the leaf carefully to avoid tears, and patch any bare spots with pieces of leaf.

1. Cut tape into rectangles and squares of various sizes. Apply tape to outside of each bowl as pattern for gold leaf.

2. On inside of bowls, apply adhesive size over taped areas with flat paintbrush. Let size dry until barely tacky.

3. When size is ready, completely cover all sized areas with gold leaf, tearing sheets as necessary.

4. With index finger or soft cloth, carefully press leaf onto glass all around bowls. Check for full coverage.

5. Let size cure about 24 hours. With soft-bristle brush, remove any leaf not adhered with adhesive size.

6. Remove tape. Burnish leaf by gently rubbing with soft cloth. To protect gilding, brush on coat of sealant. Let dry before using.

Chocolate-Covered Leaf Cake

A sweet dream for the eyes and the palate, this decorative single-layer chocolate cake will be the star attraction of any dessert table! There isn't a dessert lover anywhere who won't admire the luscious paper-thin chocolate leaves that adorn this showstopping cake. And hidden under the lovely semisweet chocolate covering is a rich chocolate cake flavored with orange liqueur and apricot jam.

What You'll Need

- ⅔ cup butter
- ¾ cup plus 1 tablespoon sugar, divided
- 4 eggs, separated, at room temperature
- 5 (1-ounce) squares semisweet chocolate, melted and cooled for 10 minutes
- 1 cup finely ground almonds
- 1 cup sifted all-purpose flour
- 6 tablespoons orange liqueur
- 2 tablespoons apricot jam, heated, strained and cooled
- 1 cup chocolate icing
- 12 rose leaves, rinsed and patted dry
- 1 teaspoon cocoa
- ½ cup heavy cream
- ½ teaspoon vanilla extract
- 1 teaspoon cream of tartar

1. Beat butter and ¾ cup sugar until light and fluffy. Stir in egg yolks, chocolate and almonds until blended.

2. Beat egg whites until stiff; gently fold whites and flour into batter. Pour into 9-inch greased springform pan; bake in a preheated 350°F oven for 45 minutes.

3. Cool cake in pan 10 minutes; remove from pan to wire rack. Prick top with fork, sprinkle with liqueur and spread with jam.

4. Melt icing in top of double boiler. Holding leaves by stems, dip 1 side into chocolate; let set on waxed paper 4 hours.

5. Let remaining icing cool, then reheat to spreading consistency. Spread icing over top and side of cake in even layer.

6. Gently peel rose leaves from chocolate leaves; discard rose leaves. Sprinkle chocolate leaves with cocoa and place decoratively in center of cake.

7. Beat together heavy cream, remaining sugar, vanilla extract and cream of tartar until stiff. Pipe rosettes around chocolate leaves; decorate each rosette with silver dragée.

Makes 1 (9-inch) cake

Rum-Flavored Cupcakes

T hese beautifully decorated, filled, rum-flavored cupcakes will delight kids and grown-ups alike. The cooled cupcakes are first halved crosswise and filled with a rich custard. After reassembly, they are frosted with the same mixture, then rolled in finely chopped toasted almonds. They are each garnished with half a candied cherry and piped with melted chocolate to resemble a flower. Packed in a lovely stenciled box, they make a special gift for any occasion.

What You'll Need

Batter

- ¾ cup sugar
- 4 tablespoons rum
- 2 large eggs
- 1 cup all-purpose flour
- ¼ teaspoon baking powder
- 3 tablespoons melted butter

Filling

- 1 cup rum
- 1 envelope unflavored gelatin
- 1 package vanilla pudding mix
- ½ cup sugar
- 1 cup whole milk
- 2 egg yolks
- 1 cup heavy cream

Garnish

- 1 cup chopped toasted almonds
- 2 ounces bittersweet chocolate, melted
- 6 candied red cherries, quartered

1. For batter, beat sugar, rum and eggs until foamy. Stir in flour and baking powder. Add butter; beat until blended.

2. Pour batter into well-greased muffin tin, filling cups ⅔ full. Bake at 400°F 30 minutes or until toothpick inserted in centers comes out clean; cool in pan 5 minutes. Remove to wire racks to cool completely.

3. For filling, combine rum and gelatin; let soften. Whisk pudding mix, sugar, milk and yolks; heat until hot.

4. Whisk gelatin mixture into pudding mixture. Remove from heat; let cool. Whip cream until stiff; fold into pudding.

5. Halve cupcakes crosswise; spread bottoms with filling. Replace tops; cover with filling. Roll sides in almonds.

6. Spoon melted chocolate into parchment cone; snip tip. Pipe stem and leaves. Place 2 cherry pieces on top of each cupcake for blossom.

Makes 12 cupcakes

Classic Linzer Torte

*U*nlike most tortes, this elegant Austrian dessert is special because of its sumptuous crust. The rich, buttery dough contains ground almonds, cocoa, cinnamon, allspice and lemon rind. A portion is used to line the inside of a springform pan, prebaked and then spread with red currant or raspberry jam. The remaining dough is cut into strips, crisscrossed over the jam, then baked until golden. More flavorful after a day or two, this torte is a special occasion in itself.

What You'll Need

- 2 cups plus 2 tablespoons all-purpose flour
- 1 teaspoon baking powder
- 1½ cups finely ground blanched almonds
- ¾ cup sugar
- 2 tablespoons cocoa
- 1 teaspoon cinnamon
- Pinch allspice
- Pinch salt
- 1 teaspoon grated lemon rind
- 14 tablespoons (1¾ sticks) unsalted butter, cut into pieces, plus extra for greasing pan
- 2 eggs
- ⅔ cup red currant or raspberry jam
- 1 egg yolk mixed with 2 tablespoons cold water

1. Combine flour, baking powder, almonds, sugar, cocoa, spices, salt and lemon rind in mixing bowl.

2. Add butter and eggs; quickly knead mixture to form dough. Preheat oven to 350°F.

3. Butter bottom and sides of 10-inch springform pan, dust lighty with flour. Roll out one-third of dough for bottom and one-third to line sides.

4. Prick bottom with fork in several places to prevent air bubbles. Bake 15 minutes.

5. Roll out remaining dough. Cut into 1-inch-thick strips; place on baking sheet. Cover; chill.

6. Spread jam evenly over slightly cooled bottom crust. Crisscross strips on top, pressing ends to secure. Brush with yolk mixture; bake 35 minutes.

Makes 1 (10-inch) torte

Child's Train Birthday Cake

Coming up with an appropriate theme for a child's birthday does not have to be daunting. For instance, this adorable train, complete with locomotive, is made from one sheet cake cut into the appropriate shapes with the help of homemade patterns, then decorated with gel icing, jelly and licorice sticks, silver dragées, colored non pareils and chocolate drops, or whatever sweet ornaments the birthday boy or girl prefers.

What You'll Need

Cake

- 1 cup (2 sticks) plus 2 tablespoons unsalted butter, plus extra for greasing pan
- ¾ cup granulated sugar
- 4 eggs
- 1 teaspoon vanilla extract
- 2¾ cups all-purpose flour
- 2 teaspoons baking powder
- 5-6 tablespoons whole milk
- 1¼ cups chopped almonds

Decoration

- Tubes of gel icing in different colors
- 1 cup confectioners' sugar mixed with 2-3 teaspoons hot water
- 1 small package *each* jelly and licorice sticks and gummy candies
- 1 small package *each* silver dragées, chocolate drops, and jimmies

1. For cake, mix all ingredients with hand mixer, occasionally scraping down side of bowl, just until blended.

2. Spread batter evenly in greased 10×15-inch baking pan. Bake in preheated 350°F oven 40 minutes. Remove cake to wire rack. Let cool in pan.

3. Draw patterns for locomotive and 4 or 5 cars on cardboard; cut out neatly.

4. Arrange patterns on cooled cake; using sharp knife, carefully cut out shapes.

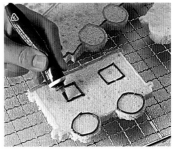

5. Use icing to outline cars, draw windows, wheels and other details on train.

6. Using sugar mixture as "glue," attach dragées to wheels, licorice sticks to windows, and other candies to decorate train appropriately.
Makes 1 cake

Decorated Cake Cover

*S*ummer is the season for outdoor dining, which brings unwelcome insects. Shield your dessert with a beautiful food cover, easily assembled from a wire lampshade frame. Large enough to protect a layer cake, the dome of finely woven fabric is adorned with silk and sheer fabric leaves and faux pearls. Its charming stem handle neatly finishes the open edge of the fabric covering. This food cover makes a lovely, practical gift.

What You'll Need

- **12" lengths of medium-weight wire**
- **Dome-shape lampshade frame, about 14" in diameter & 8½" high**
- **Spooled fine gold wire**
- **24"×48" finely woven fabric**
- **Scissors, straight pins, needle, & strong matching thread**
- **Hot-glue gun & glue sticks**
- **Silk leaves: 2 large, 8 small**
- **4 sheer fabric leaves**
- **7 large faux pearls**

— Tips & Techniques —

You can buy wire lampshade frames in craft stores, or you can recycle an old lampshade of the right dome shape. To prevent the fabric from hanging through the spokes of the frame, the spokes are encircled with three horizontal wraps of fine gold wire, secured by wrapping the wire around each individual spoke. The stem handle is shaped from lengths of sturdy wire attached to the tops of the spokes and twisted together.

1. Attach 12" length of wire to top of each spoke of lampshade frame, twisting end around each spoke to secure.

4. At top, gather fabric and wrap tightly around twisted wires to make stem handle. Turn end of fabric down.

2. Twist wires together at top. At three equal intervals, encircle frame with fine gold wire as directed in Tips.

5. From top to bottom, wrap fine gold wire tightly around fabric stem to secure. Cut and knot end of wire.

3. Center fabric over wire frame; turn bottom edge under bottom of frame. Pin, and sew on with overcast stitches.

6. Bend stem into attractive shape. Use hot glue to attach silk leaves, sheer fabric leaves, and pearls on cover.

Italian Almond Cake

At your next dinner party or family celebration, evoke a Mediterranean theme by serving this luscious Sardinian cake for dessert. Made with ground almonds and lemon rind, covered with a sweet-tart lemon icing and garnished with chopped almonds for a festive presentation, this rich cake is perfect after authentic Italian cuisine. Serve it as a special treat with a steaming espresso or dessert wine; guests will delight in your creativity.

What You'll Need

Cake

- Peel of ½ lemon
- 1 cup whole blanched almonds
- 4 eggs, separated
- ¾ cup granulated sugar
- 1½ teaspoons vanilla extract
- ½ cup all-purpose flour
- 1 teaspoon baking powder

Icing

- Juice of ½ lemon
- 1⅓ cups confectioners' sugar
- 1 teaspoon almond extract
- ½ cup chopped blanched almonds

1. Preheat oven to 350°F. For cake, finely grate lemon peel. Using nut grinder or food processor, finely grind 1 cup almonds.

2. Beat egg yolks, granulated sugar and vanilla extract in medium bowl until frothy.

3. Add lemon peel and 1 cup ground almonds to mixture; stir to combine. Sift in flour and baking powder; stir until blended.

4. Using electric beater or whisk, beat whites until stiff but not dry; gently fold into batter.

5. Grease 10-inch springform pan; dust with flour. Pour batter into pan; smooth top. Bake at 350°F 40 minutes. Remove from oven; cool.

6. For icing, combine ingredients in medium bowl; stir until smooth. Spread over cooled cake. Sprinkle ½ cup chopped almonds onto top.
Makes 1 (10-inch) cake

Little Chocolate Cakes

Wine is a component of many tasty sauces, but it is also used to enrich pastries, as with these rich, chocolatey little cakes. Butter, sugar, eggs and flour form the base of the batter, which is flavored with vanilla bean, cocoa, cinnamon and dry red wine, then fortified with mini chocolate chips. The cakes are baked, briefly cooled, then frosted with melted bittersweet chocolate. An ideal size sweet for any occasion, take them to your next tea or bridge party.

What You'll Need

- 1 cup (2 sticks) plus 5 tablespoons butter, at room temperature, plus extra for greasing
- 1 cup sugar
- 6 medium eggs
- 1 vanilla bean
- 2 cups all-purpose flour
- 2 tablespoons cocoa
- 1 teaspoon baking powder
- 1 teaspoon cinnamon
- ¼ cup dry red wine
- 4 ounces miniature chocolate chips
- Plain bread crumbs for coating forms
- 6 ounces bittersweet chocolate, melted

1. Using hand-held mixer, beat butter and sugar in large bowl until well blended and fluffy.

2. Add eggs, 1 at a time, beating after each addition. Add seeds from vanilla bean; stir.

3. Sift combined flour, baking powder, cocoa and cinnamon over egg-sugar mixture.

4. Whisk batter until well blended. Add wine; whisk. Stir in chocolate chips.

5. Grease ramekins; sprinkle with bread crumbs to coat. Fill each form ¾ full with batter.

6. Bake ramekins on baking sheet in preheated 350°F oven 25 to 30 minutes or until toothpick inserted in centers comes out clean. Cool briefly; remove from ramekins. Over wire racks, brush with melted chocolate.

Makes 10 (6-ounce) cakes

Three-Tiered Wedding Cake

This beautiful wedding cake is as memorable as it is delicious! What's more, it is surprisingly easy to make, since all the ingredients can be bought. Sponge cakes are cut to size for the tiers, brushed with plum preserves and brandy, covered with marzipan, then finished with milk chocolate icing and drizzles of white icing. Lovely sugar flowers and marzipan leaves add the perfect decorative touch.

What You'll Need

16 ounces plum preserves

6½ ounces plum brandy

3 (10-inch-round, 1½-inch-thick) prebaked layers sponge cake

10½ ounces marzipan

28 ounces milk chocolate icing

16 ounces white icing

Garnish

White or yellow sugar roses and green marzipan leaves

Mini marshmallows

Milk chocolate chips

Powdered sugar

1. In small pan, combine preserves and brandy; bring to a boil. Boil 1 minute. Cut top 2 tiers of sponge cake, one 6 inches in diameter, the other 8 inches in diameter.

2. Brush top of all 3 cake layers with warm brandy mixture; set aside 30 minutes to absorb flavoring; brush again.

3. On work surface lightly dusted with powdered sugar, roll out 3 (¼-inch-thick) circles marzipan, with diameters of 9 inches, 11 inches and 13 inches, to cover each layer. Cover each cake layer with marzipan, carefully smoothing against sides.

4. Cover each cake tier with milk chocolate icing, then drizzle with white icing. With knife, swirl icings together to marbleize.

5. Set aside layers until icing is almost set. Carefully assemble tiers, centering each tier on top of the other.

6. Decorate cake with sugar flowers, marzipan leaves, miniature marshmallows and chocolate chips; dust with powdered sugar.
Makes 1 (10-inch) tiered cake

Chocolate-Cherry Layer Cake

T*he ingredients of this ornate cake may be traditional, but its no-bake preparation is absolutely unique. With its almond-crumb base, topped with layers of plump, red sour cherries in syrup, a layer of whipped cream cheese and sour cream, then frosted with chocolate and covered with a blanket of cocoa, this cake is an extravagant creation that is sure to impress your dinner guests.*

What You'll Need

- ½ (15½-ounce) can pitted sour cherries in juice
- 2 tablespoons cornstarch mixed with 2 tablespoons water
- 4 tablespoons sugar, divided
- 6 ounces ladyfingers, crumbled
- 4 tablespoons unsalted butter, at room temperature
- 1 cup plus 1 tablespoon toasted sliced almonds, divided
- 2 ounces cream cheese, at room temperature
- ½ cup sour cream
- 6 ounces semisweet coating chocolate
- 2 tablespoons cocoa powder
- Chocolate leaves for garnish

1. In medium saucepan, bring cherries and juice to boil. Add cornstarch mixture; cook, stirring until thickened. Cool.

2. In medium bowl, mix 2 tablespoons sugar and ⅔ of ladyfinger crumbs. Add butter, and mix with your hands until beads form.

3. Press crumb mixture over bottom of 7-inch springform pan; sprinkle with ½ cup toasted almonds. Top with cherries; cover and chill 15 minutes.

4. Mix cream cheese, sour cream and remaining 2 tablespoons sugar. Spoon over cherries; spread carefully.

5. Top cake with remaining crumbs and ½ cup almonds. Melt chocolate over simmering water; frost cake in pan.

6. Sift cocoa over cake. Pipe with lattice pattern. Cover and chill at least 1 hour. Serve at room temperature, garnishing with 1 tablespoon almonds and chocolate leaves.

Makes 1 (7-inch) cake

Colorful Ribbons

Hand-painted ribbons add an elegant finishing touch to gift packages. Making them is easy: Just cut acetate stencils of a simple pattern— like the heart pattern shown here—then stencil a wide ribbon with fabric paint that coordinates with the color of your gift wrap or gift box. Tie packages or a bunch of flowers with generous bows, and give a beautiful gift to a special friend.

— Tips & Techniques —

A small heart is the basic element in the linear patterns of hearts and four-leaf clovers. Draw the designs full-size on paper and make any necessary adjustments before cutting the stencils. If you use clear acetate, you can place the pattern underneath it and trace the shape onto the acetate surface, rather than cut out the pattern to use as a template. To create this pretty package embellishment, buy solid-color ribbon and fabric paints to match your gift paper.

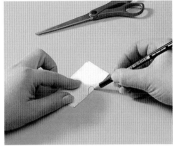

1. For one heart, fold paper in half. On fold, draw half of heart ½" tall. Cut out through both layers; open flat.

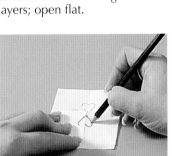

2. For cloverleaf, fold paper in quarters. Trace one heart over each fold, equidistant from center. Draw stem.

3. For radiating hearts, draw small circle. Trace row of three hearts to left and right of circle; add one circle; cut out. Draw onto acetate.

4. For alternating hearts, draw evenly spaced upright and inverted hearts; cut out. Draw onto acetate.

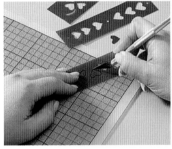

5. Working on cutting mat, cut out designs from stencil acetate using sharp craft knife.

6. Lay stencil over ribbon. With lightly loaded flat paintbrush, fill in designs with paint. When dry, move stencil and repeat.

Miniature Birthday Cake

This charming little Bundt cake is guaranteed to be a huge birthday treat. Small in size but large in impact, it is iced in pink, lovingly decorated with loads of marzipan hearts and a lush ribbon bow, and topped with a big birthday candle. Because it contains banana and sour cream, you can start the birthday celebration with this cake as part of a champagne breakfast. Bake the cake the evening before, if possible. The hardest part will be concealing its delicious aroma.

What You'll Need

Batter

- ½ **lemon**
- 1 **large ripe banana**
- ⅓ **cup sour cream**
- 7 **tablespoons butter, softened**
- ½ **cup granulated sugar**
- 1 **teaspoon vanilla**
-   **Pinch salt**
- 2 **eggs**
- 1⅓ **cups all-purpose flour**
- 1½ **teaspoons baking powder**

Decoration

- 2 **tablespoons raspberry syrup**
- 1 **tablespoon hot water**
- 2 **cups powdered sugar, divided**
- 7 **ounces marzipan**
-   **Red food coloring**

1. From lemon, grate peel and squeeze juice. In small bowl, blend mixture with banana and sour cream; set aside.

2. With mixer, whip butter, granulated sugar, vanilla and salt in large bowl until fluffy.

3. Stir in eggs, 1 at a time, then sift flour and baking powder over mixture; mix until just blended. Blend in banana mixture. Grease and lightly flour 7-inch Bundt pan.

4. Pour batter into Bundt pan. With spatula, smooth top. Bake in preheated 375°F oven about 50 minutes.

5. Combine raspberry syrup, hot water and 1¼ cups powdered sugar; stir until smooth. Ice cake.

6. Knead marzipan with remaining ¾-cup sugar and food coloring. Roll out between 2 sheets plastic wrap to ⅛-inch thickness. Cut hearts with small cookie cutter; decorate cake.
Makes 1 (7-inch) cake

Lavender Cream Cake

Lavender has been used in perfumes and sachets for centuries. Some cultures also use it as a flavoring for everything from tea to ice cream. Try the delicate flavor of lavender in this luscious no-bake cream cake, which has been flavored with a simple lavender infusion and aromatic lavender honey to sweeten the rich mousselike whipped cream and cheese filling. Topped off with sugared lavender sprigs, this is a perfect dessert for any occasion.

What You'll Need

- 3 tablespoons untreated lavender blossoms
- 8 ounces plain vanilla cookies
- ¾ cup (1½ sticks) unsalted butter
- 1 (8-ounce) package cream cheese, at room temperature
- ½ cup lavender honey
- 1¼ cups whipping cream, well chilled

1. Place lavender blossoms in small bowl. Add 3 tablespoons boiling water; steep about 15 minutes. Cool.

2. Place cookies in large, plastic zip-tight bag. Crush with rolling pin to form coarse crumbs.

3. Melt butter and let cool. Combine cookie crumbs and butter in medium bowl; stir until thoroughly mixed.

4. Beginning in center, press crumb mixture into 9-inch springform pan; cover bottom evenly.

5. Strain lavender infusion. Beat cream cheese and honey until blended. Add cooled infusion; beat until smooth.

6. Beat whipping cream until stiff. Gently fold into filling mixture. Pour into pan; spread evenly over crumbs. Chill until firm, at least 3 to 4 hours before serving.

Makes 1 (9-inch) cake

Charlotte with Vanilla Cream

I t should come as no surprise that this elegant molded dessert, called a charlotte, is a French classic. It is a bit time-consuming to prepare, but requires no special techniques. A jelly-roll cake is spread with raspberry jam, rolled up and cut into slices used to line a deep bowl. A rich vanilla cream is poured into the cake-lined bowl and chilled. After it is unmolded, the charlotte is garnished with fresh raspberries and cream for a dazzling presentation.

What You'll Need

Cake

- 4 eggs, separated
- 2 tablespoons water
- 1 teaspoon vanilla
- ½ cup granulated sugar
- Pinch salt
- ½ cup plus 1 tablespoon all-purpose flour
- 2 tablespoons cornstarch
- Pinch baking powder
- Powdered sugar
- 1 cup seedless raspberry jam

Filling

- 1 cup milk
- 1 vanilla bean, split lengthwise
- 8 sheets unflavored gelatin, softened in cold water and squeezed out
- 4 egg yolks
- ½ cup granulated sugar
- 1 pint heavy cream
- Fresh raspberries for garnish

1. In medium mixing bowl, beat egg yolks, water, vanilla, ¼ cup sugar and salt until foamy. Preheat oven to 450°F.

2. Whisk in flour, cornstarch and baking powder. Beat egg whites with remaining ¼ cup sugar until stiff; fold in.

3. Spread batter evenly in jelly-roll pan; bake 8 minutes. Turn out cake onto kitchen towel sprinkled with powdered sugar. Cool slightly.

4. Spread cake with jam; roll up. Line bowl with plastic wrap, and then with slices of jelly roll.

5. Bring milk and vanilla to a boil; cool. Add gelatin. Beat yolks and sugar until foamy. Whisk into milk to form custard.

6. Whip cream; fold into custard. Pour into cake-lined bowl; cover with cake slices. Chill 2 hours or until set and ready to serve. Garnish with fresh raspberries and whipped cream.

Makes 6 to 8 servings

Black Forest Cake

A classic combination of chocolate, cherries and whipped cream, black forest cake is a tour de force that makes any occasion a special one. Easily assembled from a store-bought cake that is cut into three layers and moistened with cherry juice and brandy, it is filled with homemade cherry sauce and whipped cream, then covered with more whipped cream and chocolate sprinkles. To complete the stunning presentation, piped whipped cream stars are each topped with a plump cherry.

What You'll Need

- 1 chocolate cake, at least 9 inches in diameter
- 3 tablespoons cherry brandy
- 1 (16 ounce) can sweet cherries, drained and juice reserved
- 2 teaspoons cream of tartar mixed with 2 tablespoons cherry juice
- 2 cups (1 pint) whipping cream
- 2 tablespoons powdered sugar
- 4 tablespoons chocolate sprinkles

1. If necessary, cut cake to 9-inch diameter, then cut horizontally into 3 layers.

2. Sprinkle each layer with 1 tablespoon brandy. Bring 1 cup cherry juice to a boil. Stir in cream of tartar mixture.

3. Cook juice, whisking, until thick. Stir in all but 16 cherries; remove from heat. Whip cream and sugar.

4. Place 1 layer in 9-inch springform pan. Spread with ½ of cherry filling and ¼ of whipped cream.

5. Top with second cake layer. Repeat cherry filling and whipped cream. Top with third layer.

6. Cover cake with whipped cream and sprinkles. Pipe whipped cream stars around edge; top each star with reserved cherry.

Makes 1 (9 inch) cake

Stamped Wrapping Paper

*L*inoleum block printing is an established art form. Here it is simplified using stamps with clever cork handles to decorate wrapping paper and gift tags. Rather than pressing the stamp into ink, as with rubber stamping, you apply the paint or ink to this stamp with a paint roller. Select the motifs to suit the occasion or the recipient's taste. Stamping turns even humble parcel paper into impressive gift wrap.

What You'll Need

Pencil & heavy paper

Scissors

Piece of unmounted linoleum

Linoleum cutting tool

Sharp knife

Bottle cork

Strong glue or hot-glue gun & glue stick

Acrylic or block-printing paint or ink

Pane of glass (with smooth edges)

4"-wide paint roller

Solid-color wrapping paper

— Tips & Techniques —

Unmounted linoleum, about ⅛" thick, can be cut to size with a sharp knife or paper trimmer. The cutting tool has a handle and assorted cutters that fit into it. You will need at least one narrow and one wide cutter, and they must be sharp. Simple graphic designs work best for the stamp. Remember that the motif will be reversed when it is stamped.

1. Select motif for stamp and draw it on heavy paper, or trace motif from book or other source. Cut out motif carefully.

2. Lay cutout motif on corner of right side of unmounted linoleum. Outline motif with pencil.

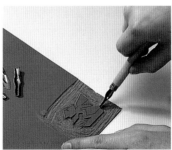

3. With cutting tool, carefully remove all linoleum that is not part of design to be printed.

4. With sharp knife, cut linoleum a little bigger all around than the design. Glue cork to center back of linoleum.

5. Pour some paint onto pane of glass. Roll paint roller through paint, then onto stamp to apply thin coat of paint.

6. Using even pressure, stamp motif randomly over wrapping paper. Reapply paint and repeat. Let dry completely before wrapping.

Anniversary Cake

S how that special person how much you care by acknowledging an important day with a lovely cake topped with iced cookie hearts that carry your loving sentiments. With the help of a cake mix and ready-made cookie dough, you can whip it up in almost no time. A simple rum-and-sugar icing that is dyed several shades of pink is used to glaze the cake and the heart-shaped cookies, which are embellished with decorating gel. This cake says "I love you" in more ways than one.

What You'll Need

- 1 package ready-made sugar cookie dough
- Heart-shaped cookie cutters in various sizes
- 2 cups powdered sugar, divided
- 5 tablespoons white rum or cherry juice, divided
- Red food coloring
- 1 tube *each* red, white and pink decorating gel
- 1 cake mix, plus required ingredients listed on package

1. Roll out cookie dough to ¼-inch thickness. Cut out hearts. Bake according to package instructions.

2. Mix ¾ cup sugar with 2 tablespoons rum; coat 1 cookie. Tint icing pale pink; use to coat 2 to 3 cookies. Let set on wire rack.

Darken glaze; coat maining cookies. Let set on rack. With gel, write es on cookies.

4. Mix and bake cake according to package instructions. Let cool and remove from pan; cool completely.

5. Add remaining 3 tablespoons rum and 1 cup sugar to glaze. Brush crumbs from cake; cover with glaze. Let set.

6. Add remaining ¼ cup sugar to thicken glaze. Dab backs of cookies with glaze and attach to cake.
Makes 1 (9- to 10-inch) cake

Cream-Filled Chocolate Cake

*T*his scrumptious cream-
filled chocolate layer
cake is a grand finale for any
special occasion. And because
it's made with purchased or
premade cake layers, it
leaves time for other party
preparations. Filled with a
luscious mixture of whipped
cream and cranberry preserves,
frosted with a glistening
chocolate ganache and
beautifully garnished with
florettes and chocolate candies,
this cake is sure to win raves.

- 8 ounces good-quality semisweet chocolate
- 4 cups (2 pints) whipping cream, well chilled, divided
- 1 teaspoon cinnamon
- ½ teaspoon ground coriander
- Large pinch ground cloves
- 2 tablespoons powdered sugar
- 2 teaspoons vanilla
- 8 ounces cranberry or red currant preserves
- 1 envelope unflavored gelatin, mixed with 2 tablespoons water
- 3 (9-inch) purchased or premade chocolate cake layers
- Chocolate candy ornaments for garnish

1. To make ganache, heat chocolate and 1 cup cream, stirring, until melted. Stir in spices; cover and chill until of spreading consistency.

4. Spread layer with half of cream filling. Repeat with second layer. Top with third layer. Cover and refrigerate at least 3 hours or until cream has set.

2. Beat 1½ cups and vanilla until in preserves, res 2 tablespoons f

5. Beat ganache. Whip 1 cup cream until stiff; fold into nache until blended. Remove from cake.

3. Heat ge gelatin ha cream mi layer into

3.
rem
wire
messag

Creamy Strawberry Cake

This delightful cake exudes Victorian romance and is the ultimate tea party charmer. Its puff pastry layers, filled with hazelnut meringue and sweet strawberry cream, and topped with grated white chocolate and sugar roses and leaves, make this cake a welcome addition to any spring table. Surround the cake with dyed eggs and candy bunnies, and you've got a splendid finale dessert for your Easter dinner.

What You'll Need

Pastry

- 2 (17¼ ounce) packages frozen puff pastry, thawed
- 1 egg white
- ¼ cup sugar
- ½ cup ground hazelnuts

Filling

- 2 cups (1 pint) strawberries
- 8 ounces mascarpone cheese
- ⅓ cup sugar
- Juice of 1 lemon
- 2 tablespoons rum
- 1 envelope unflavored gelatin
- 2 cups (1 pint) whipping cream

Decoration

- 2 ounces white baking chocolate
- Sugar roses and leaves

1. On a floured surface with a floured rolling pin, roll 1 sheet of thawed puff pastry into 9½x19-inch rectangle. Fold rectangle in half to make a square. With a pastry wheel or sharp knife, cut around 9-inch cake pan to make 1 pastry circle. Repeat this with 2 more sheets to make 3 circles in all. Preheat oven to 350°F; bake crusts 15 minutes.

2. With mixer at high speed, beat egg white until stiff peaks form, adding sugar gradually. Fold in ground hazelnuts.

3. On parchment-lined baking sheet, spread each crust with one-third of meringue. Bake 15 minutes at 350°F.

4. Wash strawberries; purée in blender. Mix with mascarpone, sugar, lemon juice and rum.

5. Mix gelatin as label directs; fold into strawberry mixture. Whip cream until stiff; fold into strawberries.

6. Chill cream 2 hours. Spread each pastry circle with one-third of cream; stack circles.

7. Grate white baking chocolate over top of cake. Decorate with sugar roses and leaves.
Makes 1 (9-inch) cake

Children's Zoo Cake

*S*urprise and delight a birthday girl or boy with this playfully decorated zoo cake. A butter-rich cake batter is smoothed over a hidden bottom of pineapple rings and cherries swathed in butter and brown sugar, then baked until golden. The cooled cake is covered with white icing to create a canvas for a zoo of piped green and chocolate icing that will house a menagerie of gummy candy animals.

What You'll Need

- 1¼ cups (2½ sticks) **unsalted butter, divided**
- ½ cup **brown sugar**
- 2 (20-ounce) cans **sliced pineapple rings**
- 2 (9-ounce) cans **pitted dark, sweet cherries**
- 10 **egg yolks**
- 1 cup **granulated sugar**
- **Grated rind of 1 lemon**
- 10 **egg whites and pinch of salt, stiffly beaten**
- 3½ cups **all-purpose flour**
- 2 teaspoons **baking powder**
- **White, green and chocolate icing**
- **Assorted gummy candy animals**

1. Melt 5 tablespoons butter; brush over sheet cake pan. Sprinkle with brown sugar to evenly cover pan.

2. Arrange pineapple rings in single layer in pan; place cherry in center of each ring. Melt remaining butter.

3. Mix butter, yolks, granulated sugar and lemon rind. Gently fold in beaten whites, flour and baking powder.

4. With rubber spatula, gently spread batter evenly over fruit without disturbing arrangement.

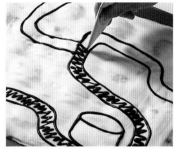

5. Bake on middle rack of preheated 350°F oven for 60 to 65 minutes, until toothpick inserted in center comes out clean. Let cool; cover with white icing. Draw path, cages, and trees with chocolate icing.

6. Fill treetops with green icing. Frost animals' backs, press gently into the cake, and let set before cutting into squares.

Makes 1 sheet cake

Index

Notes

Notes

METRIC CONVERSION CHART

VOLUME MEASUREMENTS (dry)

$^1/_8$ teaspoon = 0.5 mL
$^1/_4$ teaspoon = 1 mL
$^1/_2$ teaspoon = 2 mL
$^3/_4$ teaspoon = 4 mL
1 teaspoon = 5 mL
1 tablespoon = 15 mL
2 tablespoons = 30 mL
$^1/_4$ cup = 60 mL
$^1/_3$ cup = 75 mL
$^1/_2$ cup = 125 mL
$^2/_3$ cup = 150 mL
$^3/_4$ cup = 175 mL
1 cup = 250 mL
2 cups = 1 pint = 500 mL
3 cups = 750 mL
4 cups = 1 quart = 1 L

VOLUME MEASUREMENTS (fluid)

1 fluid ounce (2 tablespoons) = 30 mL
4 fluid ounces ($^1/_2$ cup) = 125 mL
8 fluid ounces (1 cup) = 250 mL
12 fluid ounces (1$^1/_2$ cups) = 375 mL
16 fluid ounces (2 cups) = 500 mL

WEIGHTS (mass)

$^1/_2$ ounce = 15 g
1 ounce = 30 g
3 ounces = 90 g
4 ounces = 120 g
8 ounces = 225 g
10 ounces = 285 g
12 ounces = 360 g
16 ounces = 1 pound = 450 g

DIMENSIONS

$^1/_{16}$ inch = 2 mm
$^1/_8$ inch = 3 mm
$^1/_4$ inch = 6 mm
$^1/_2$ inch = 1.5 cm
$^3/_4$ inch = 2 cm
1 inch = 2.5 cm

OVEN TEMPERATURES

250°F = 120°C
275°F = 140°C
300°F = 150°C
325°F = 160°C
350°F = 180°C
375°F = 190°C
400°F = 200°C
425°F = 220°C
450°F = 230°C

BAKING PAN SIZES

Utensil	Size in Inches/Quarts	Metric Volume	Size in Centimeters
Baking or Cake Pan (square or rectangular)	8 × 8 × 2	2 L	20 × 20 × 5
	9 × 9 × 2	2.5 L	23 × 23 × 5
	12 × 8 × 2	3 L	30 × 20 × 5
	13 × 9 × 2	3.5 L	33 × 23 × 5
Loaf Pan	8 × 4 × 3	1.5 L	20 × 10 × 7
	9 × 5 × 3	2 L	23 × 13 × 7
Round Layer Cake Pan	8 × 1$^1/_2$	1.2 L	20 × 4
	9 × 1$^1/_2$	1.5 L	23 × 4
Pie Plate	8 × 1$^1/_4$	750 mL	20 × 3
	9 × 1$^1/_4$	1 L	23 × 3
Baking Dish or Casserole	1 quart	1 L	—
	1$^1/_2$ quart	1.5 L	—
	2 quart	2 L	—